It is only with the heart that one can see rightly; what is essential is invisible to the eye.

—Antoine de Saint-Exupéry

**MIRACLES &
MYSTERIES
of MERCY
HOSPITAL**

MIRACLES & MYSTERIES
of MERCY HOSPITAL

Pain Relief

BETH ADAMS

Miracles & Mysteries of Mercy Hospital is a trademark of Guideposts.

Published by Guideposts Books & Inspirational Media
100 Reserve Road, Suite E200
Danbury, CT 06810
Guideposts.org

Copyright © 2022 by Guideposts. All rights reserved.

This book, or parts thereof, may not be reproduced, stored in a retrieval system, or transmitted in any form or by any means, electronic, mechanical, photocopying, recording, or otherwise, without the written permission of the publisher.

This is a work of fiction. While the setting of Mercy Hospital as presented in this series is fictional, the location of Charleston, South Carolina, actually exists, and some places and characters may be based on actual places and people whose identities have been used with permission or fictionalized to protect their privacy. Apart from the actual people, events, and locales that figure into the fiction narrative, all other names, characters, businesses, and events are the creation of the author's imagination and any resemblance to actual persons or events is coincidental.

Every attempt has been made to credit the sources of copyrighted material used in this book. If any such acknowledgment has been inadvertently omitted or miscredited, receipt of such information would be appreciated.

Scripture references are from the following sources: *The Holy Bible, King James Version* (KJV). *The Holy Bible, New International Version* (NIV). Copyright © 1973, 1978, 1984, 2011 by Biblica, Inc. Used by permission of Zondervan. All rights reserved worldwide. www.zondervan.com.

Cover and interior design by Müllerhaus
Cover illustration by Bob Kayganich, represented by Illustration Online LLC.
Typeset by Aptara, Inc.

Printed and bound in the United States of America
10 9 8 7 6 5 4 3 2 1

Pain Relief

Chapter One

ANNE MABRY LOVED DELIVERING FLOWERS to the maternity ward. She loved the excitement that was always in the air, the tiny babies swaddled in blankets, the joy that permeated the whole floor. Each bouquet of flowers she delivered was a celebration that a new baby had just been born—a new life had entered the world, and the new little person's family and friends were rejoicing. Today she carried a gorgeous bouquet of pink lilies, which Anne was pretty sure were from her friend Joy's own garden. Joy was a master gardener and often brought in flowers she'd grown herself to include in the bouquets sold in the hospital's gift shop. The lilies gave off the most heavenly scent, and they would brighten any hospital room.

This bouquet of flowers was to be delivered to... Anne checked the card again. Room 321. Toward the end, then. She smiled as she walked down the hallway, and she waved at her friend Shirley Bashore as she passed the nurses' station. She edged to the side as another nurse wheeled a bassinet past her, and then she ducked to the other side of the hallway as Luke Merritt, a member of the transport team, pushed two empty wheelchairs toward the elevators. A woman was taking pictures of a couple posing with a newborn just ahead. Anne nodded at two doctors, chatting as they walked past in white coats. She smiled at a woman—a new grandmother, Anne guessed—holding a tiny squalling infant carefully in her arms as she wandered up and down the hallway. Finally, Anne made it to room 321, and she knocked gently on the partially closed door.

"Come in," someone called from inside. Anne pushed on the door gently and held out the flowers as she walked in. "Celeste Wright?" She smiled at the woman sitting up in the bed.

"Yes." The woman's long hair was disheveled, and the dark half moons under her eyes betrayed her exhaustion, but she still looked blissfully, radiantly happy as she held a nursing infant against her. A man lay on the couch by the windows, shirt rumpled, glasses askew, a bewildered smile on his face.

"Special delivery," Anne said. She set the vase down on the console by the bed. "Congratulations." It always seemed impossible that newborn babies were really this small. This one had a full head of dark hair and the cone-shaped head that often signaled that the birth had been difficult. It would return to its normal shape soon. "Your baby is beautiful."

"Thank you. She is gorgeous, isn't she?" Celeste nodded at the flowers. "Who are they from? Do you mind checking?"

"Not at all. You've got your hands full." Anne leaned in to read the little white card attached to the stems. "We're so happy for you and can't wait to meet Caroline Lily. Love, Momma and Daddy." Anne smiled. "Aw, lilies for Caroline Lily."

"That's nice," Celeste said. She looked down at the baby. "Did you hear that, little peanut? Your grandparents can't wait to meet you."

"Is there anything you need?" Anne asked, moving toward the door.

"No, we're good," Celeste said.

Anne slipped out of the room, leaving the new parents to tend to their baby. Those first few days were overwhelming and exhausting and wonderful all at once. She walked back down the hallway, cringing as somewhere nearby a woman cried out in pain. Labor was miserable, but it was so worth it. Anne passed a number of rooms and the small waiting area for families and the bathrooms. She waved at Olga Dotov, a member of the custodial staff, pushing her cart away from the recovery room. And up ahead—wait.

Anne couldn't have seen that right. She backed up and looked into the open doorway of the C-section recovery room. Was that...?

Anne stepped inside. The room was empty. It was often empty, as it was only used by patients who had just had a caesarean birth, and they didn't perform too many of those here at Mercy Hospital. But there at the end, just in the sight line of the doorway, was a medication machine. Anne didn't know all the details about how it worked, but she knew that when a doctor prescribed something for a patient, a nurse was able to log in and enter their credentials, and the drawers on the machine would slide open so the item could be retrieved and given out. It was roughly the size of the industrial copier they'd used in the St. Michael's church office, but instead of paper, the drawers were filled with drugs. The drawers should have been closed, except when a nurse was taking medication out. It was supposed to be a very secure way to dispense and track prescriptions. So why were several of the drawers standing open right now, when no one was in the room?

She stepped closer. Three…no, four of the machine's drawers were open, and two of them had shards of plastic broken off at the top, as if…well, Anne wasn't even sure what. She peered inside the first drawer, and instead of the rotating carousel that dispensed the right medication, she saw mangled plastic, as well as a bunch of small white pills. What in the world…? Anne straightened up and saw that the screen on the machine showed a blinking red ERROR!

Someone had broken into it and taken medication from inside. But how? And who? And which ones were gone? Anne wasn't sure, but she did know that she had to tell someone—right away. She turned and hurried out of the room and back down the hall to the nurses' station. Shirley was still there, thank goodness, typing something on one of the computers lining the long desk.

"Shirley!" Anne said. "The machine! Someone broke into it."

"What?" Shirley looked up, her eyes narrowed. Another nurse sitting next to her—Anne thought her name was Gina—looked up too. "Which machine?"

"The medicine one," Anne said. "With drawers?"

"The Pyxis?" Shirley looked over at Gina, who was already pushing her chair back.

"Yes. That one. The one in the C-section recovery room."

"Show us," Shirley said, standing. Anne nodded and started off, Shirley and Gina following just a step behind. They hurried to the recovery room, and when they got to the doorway, Shirley gasped. She rushed forward to examine the broken drawers.

"Oh my goodness," Gina said softly.

"It looks like someone jimmied them open somehow," Anne said.

"It does indeed," Shirley said. "And it looks like…" She let her voice trail off.

"Demerol?" Gina asked. "That's usually in this drawer." She tapped the closest one to her. "And oxycodone."

"This one is hydromorphone and hydrocodone," Shirley said, shaking her head.

"Fentanyl," Gina added.

The names sounded familiar to Anne. "Are those drugs for pain?"

"Those are all powerful opioids," Shirley confirmed. "And they've been cleaned out. Someone broke into this machine and took a huge amount of dangerous opioid medications."

The next fifteen minutes were a blur, as security and hospital administration were called in and Shirley and Gina blocked off the recovery room. "In case whoever did this left fingerprints behind," Shirley explained. Anne knew it was also important to make sure no one accessed the medication that remained in the open drawers. Whatever it was, it could be dangerous if taken in the wrong circumstances.

"Tell me what you saw," Garrison Baker asked Anne again as several members of the hospital administration swarmed around the machine. Anne had already told Paige, the charge nurse on shift today, but she repeated the story, such as it was.

"Did you see anyone in the area?" he asked when she finished.

"There were people all around," Anne said. "It's always busy here."

Anne repeated her story to the police a few minutes later, first to Officer Escobar and after that, to Detective Albert Lee.

"What time did you find the machine open?" Detective Lee asked. The police had set up a temporary command station in an unused delivery room, and he was seated on a swivel stool by the computer. Anne sat awkwardly on the bed, as if she were being examined—and it felt like she was.

"I didn't check my watch, but I would guess it was around twelve thirty or so. I had just come back from my lunch break when Aurora assigned me to deliver flowers."

"When was the last time you were in that recovery room?"

"It's been months. Maybe years. I don't go into the rooms like that, where they're dealing with patients just out of surgery. I'm not a medical professional or anything, just a volunteer."

"Is there more than one door to the recovery room?"

"I believe there's just the one that goes to the hallway, but you may need to ask a doctor or nurse to be sure."

"Who else was in the area at the time?"

"There were so many people all around," Anne said.

"Tell me the names of anyone you remember seeing." Detective Lee took notes in a little black notebook, and he peered up at Anne through thick-framed glasses. Anne had worked with him before, and he was a nice guy. If he came across as a bit intense...well, this was an intense situation.

"Okay." Anne thought back. "Well, I saw Olga right before I noticed the drawers were open. She was just outside the recovery room."

"What's her role?"

"She's on custodial."

"She cleans the rooms?"

"And empties the trash. Strips and remakes beds. That kind of thing."

"When you saw her, had she come from inside the room with the machine?"

"I don't know. It's possible, but I didn't see." Anne wanted to be careful to speak accurately, given the stakes here.

"Who else?"

"Well, I had just come from delivering flowers to a woman down in 321. Celeste. But she was in bed holding her baby."

"We'll be interviewing all the patients on the floor to see if they saw anything," Detective Lee said. "For now, let's focus on anyone you saw in the hallway or near the room with the machine."

"Okay. Um, I remember there was a baby being wheeled to the nursery. I don't know the name of the nurse who was pushing the bassinet, but it wouldn't be hard to find out."

"We'll figure out who that was." Detective Lee made a note in his notebook.

"I saw Shirley and a few of the other nurses when I went past the nurses' station," Anne continued. "Gina was there the first time. And Kitty as well. But there were probably other nurses out on the floor, tending to patients."

"We'll interview everyone who was on duty. Anyone else?"

Anne closed her eyes and thought. "Wait. There was the transport. Luke Merritt. I saw him pushing a couple of wheelchairs."

"A transport is…"

"An employee who moves things," Anne said. "They bring patients and equipment from place to place throughout the hospital."

"Got it. Does Luke work on this floor usually?"

"He works all over the hospital," Anne said. "They all do."

"Anyone else?"

"Not that I can think of specifically. But like I said, there were a lot of people around."

He nodded, scribbling something on the page. "When did you go into the recovery room?"

"When I saw that the drawers were open."

"How long were you in the room?"

"I don't know. Maybe a minute? Probably less. I just saw that something looked odd and went to go check it out. As soon as I realized what was wrong, I told Shirley."

"How quickly would you say you moved, once you realized something was wrong?"

"As quickly as I could." Why was he looking at her like that? "I don't think it took me thirty seconds, if that." He didn't really believe…

"Remind me what your duties at the hospital are?"

"I'm a volunteer, so I do whatever Aurora Kingston, the volunteer coordinator, assigns me to do. Often it's delivering flowers, like today. Sometimes I do patient discharge, or I fill in at the front desk. Whatever needs to be done."

"So you roam around the hospital at will?"

"Not at will. Like I said, I do whatever task I'm assigned. But I do get to see many different parts of the hospital, yes."

"Do you ever have access to the Pyx—" He glanced down at his notes. "The Pyxis machines?"

"No. You have to log in to use the system. It checks your fingerprint and everything. Only people who need to access the medications can. I don't have anything to do with dispensing medicine, so I can't."

"But you know what the machines do and where they are and roughly how to use them?"

Anne hesitated. He couldn't sincerely think she had anything to do with this, could he? "I've probably seen most of them, but I honestly couldn't tell you where they are. I don't really pay attention to them, since, like I said, I can't access the medication. And I'm unsure how they work, beyond the basics."

"Why don't you tell me what you know."

Anne nodded. "I believe that when a doctor prescribes a medication for a patient, the pharmacy department enters that into the server that runs all the connected machines. As soon as it's in the system, a nurse can log in and enter the patient number, and the Pyxis machine's drawer will pop open so they can take the drug out and administer it to the patient. The machines are restocked by the pharmacy regularly."

"They're like vending machines but for extremely powerful and addictive medication?" Detective Lee's head was cocked.

"In some cases," Anne said. "I don't think all the medicine in them is addictive. I don't really know."

"So you don't know what medicine is stored in the machine?"

"I assume it's the basics. Whatever is needed. I've never really thought about it. Gina and Shirley said that the medicine that was taken today was all opioids."

He scribbled on his notepad as she spoke.

"Do you have any idea who might have wanted to get into the machine?"

"No. If they were right that opioids were taken, I suppose there are plenty of people who might want to get to those." Anne stuffed down the twinge of dread she felt. "I know those are easily abused."

"Do you know if any of the people you saw on the floor today might have reason to want to get their hands on opioids?"

Anne wasn't sure what to say. Did she think any of the people she'd seen in the hospital this afternoon abused opioids? "I really wouldn't know," she said. "I hope not."

"Have you ever used opioids?"

"What?" She shook her head. "I mean, after a gallbladder surgery many years ago, they gave me a prescription for Vicodin, but I didn't end up using them all. Not since then."

He was still eyeing her. "Can you think of anything else you'd like to tell me about what you saw today?"

Anne couldn't tell what he wanted her to say. He seemed to think she could have done it, or else knew who did. If she was aware of who had broken into the machine, didn't he think she would say so?

"If I remember anything else, I'll be sure to let you know," she said.

Detective Lee looked down at his pages of notes and nodded. "Right. I have your contact information. I'll give you a call if I have any more questions. Don't leave the area, please."

"Like, the area of the hospital?"

"Charleston. Just in case we need to talk to you again."

He thought she might leave town? Was he for real? Did he honestly think she could be responsible?

A few people looked at Anne as she walked out of the room. She saw Shirley, who beckoned to her.

"I've got texts from both Evelyn and Joy, asking what's going on in the maternity ward," Shirley said. "I bet you do too."

Anne's cell phone was tucked into the pocket of her sweater, but it was set to silent. She pulled it out and glanced at the screen. Shirley was right—she had messages from Joy and Evelyn, who, along with Shirley, were Anne's closest friends at the hospital.

"I have my lunch break in a few minutes," Shirley said. "Do you have some time to meet up with them and fill them in on what happened?"

"I do. Have you already spoken with the police?"

"I talked to Rebekah while you were in with Detective Lee. I didn't have a lot to say, so it went quick."

"Great. Want to tell Joy and Evelyn we'll meet them at the coffee shop in ten?"

"Sounds good."

Anne went to the volunteer center to check in with Aurora and let her know she would be taking a break. Aurora had heard about the theft and wanted the full story from Anne, so by the time Anne made it down to the coffee shop on the first floor, her friends were all there, gathered around one of the round tables.

"We got you a cup of coffee," Joy said, gesturing at the paper cup on the table.

"Thank you." Anne slipped into the empty chair, and as soon as she sat down, a weight she hadn't known she'd been carrying seemed to slip off her shoulders. It had been a trying few hours, but it felt good to be here with her friends.

"So." Evelyn, who was the head of the records department, leaned in. "The rumor is that someone broke into a Pyxis machine, and you were the one who discovered it."

"Wow." Anne took a sip of the coffee, and the dark rich brew tasted like heaven. "It never ceases to amaze me how fast news travels around this hospital."

"How long have you been volunteering here?" Joy asked, cocking her head. "Surely you understand that people know every little thing that happens within these walls by now."

"So what happened?" Evelyn asked.

Anne recounted the story again, and Shirley filled in the list of medication that was kept in the drawers that had been opened. "Demerol, oxycodone, hydromorphone, fentanyl, and hydrocodone," Shirley said. Anne had heard the list enough times in the past hour that she could probably recite it herself. She also now knew that oxycodone was often called by the brand name Oxycontin and hydrocodone was often known as Vicodin. Demerol was a brand name too, though hydromorphone and fentanyl were usually called by their generic names.

"Those are serious drugs." Evelyn sipped her coffee. Her silver hair was pulled into a messy knot at the back of her head, and a pencil was stuck through it to hold it in place. "Opioids."

"Someone knew what they were looking for," Shirley agreed. "Whoever it was knew exactly what they wanted and where to find it."

"Which would imply the thief was familiar with the machine," Joy said. "It's got to be someone who knows the Pyxis and the drugs inside it pretty well."

"I would imagine anyone willing to break into a Pyxis machine would be someone who was familiar with those particular drugs," Shirley said.

"But wouldn't someone who knew the machine well just, you know, open it the normal way?" Evelyn asked. "Why break into it?" She turned to Anne. "You said the drawers were just standing open?"

"They were pried open," Anne said, nodding. "At least that's how it seemed. The plastic on the tops of the drawers was broken and bent, like someone had used a lot of force to get them open."

"Pried open with what?" Evelyn asked.

Anne shrugged. "I don't know. I suppose that's one of the things the police will be looking into. But that doesn't answer the question of why they had to be pried open."

"That's easy," Shirley said. "It's because when you use the machine the normal way, there's a record. The system tracks who uses it, what they take out, how often they access it, all of that."

"We have records of every time a Pyxis is accessed," Evelyn confirmed.

"So you couldn't, say, access the machine to get a painkiller for a patient and take a few extra for yourself?" Anne asked. "The machine would know that?"

"Technically, yes, you could," Shirley said. "Say you went to the machine to get Demerol for a patient. Maybe someone recovering from a C-section, for instance. The doctor prescribes it, and a nurse would then log into the machine, enter the patient number, select the prescribed medication, and the drawer on the machine would slide open. There's a carousel inside with several different kinds of medication, and it would slide around to give you access to the one you want."

"So even though there are different kinds of medicine in the drawer, you can only get to one?" Anne asked.

Shirley nodded. "We take out the prescribed number of pills, but then we have to count the number left in the drawer and enter that number into the machine. That's how it tracks what's there—by what we tell the machine is left in the compartment."

"So theoretically, someone could access the compartment for Demerol, take an extra pill or two, but tell the machine there was still the expected number left."

"That's right," Shirley said.

"The next time the pharmacy refilled the machine, wouldn't someone realize the count was off, though?" Joy asked.

"Sure." Anne nodded, understanding. "But assuming several nurses access the medicine throughout the day, there would be no way to know which one took the extra."

"So someone theoretically could skim medication from the machine without getting caught," Joy said.

Shirley pressed her lips together but didn't answer.

"What?" Anne recognized that look on Shirley's face. There was something she wasn't saying.

"The count has been off several times recently," Shirley finally said. "More than it should be."

"You mean, someone has been taking drugs from the machine?" Joy asked.

"I don't know for sure," Shirley said. "And I don't know who. I just know that the pill count has been off enough times in recent months that I reported it, and I know Garrison said the hospital was looking into it."

"He asked for the past several months of Pyxis records for the floor last week," Evelyn confirmed.

"Who was it?" Anne felt a rush of excitement. "Whoever it is, that's got to be the person who did this."

"I honestly don't know who it is," Shirley said. "Or if it's only one person. Maybe someone—or multiple people—have simply made a series of errors. I couldn't say. I just know that the hospital is aware that the count has been off enough to raise suspicions."

"We need to figure out who it is," Anne repeated. "That's got to be the person who did this."

"Maybe," Evelyn said.

"Why would a person who has been stealing medicine the way you describe suddenly change tactics, though?" Joy asked. "If they've been getting away with it that way, why suddenly break into the machine today?"

"It sounds like they haven't exactly been getting away with it," Anne said, "if the hospital knows it's been happening."

"But the hospital doesn't know who it is," Joy said. "So they haven't been caught yet."

"Maybe the person knows they're about to be caught." Truthfully, Anne understood Joy's point. But she also saw that this was too much of a connection to simply be a coincidence. "Maybe they heard the hospital was looking into it. They were getting nervous, so they decided to change tactics and take a lot at once instead of one or two at a time."

"But what happened today was so much more dangerous. You'd risk being caught," Joy said. "Right? I mean, anyone could have walked in on the person in the process."

"That's what makes this particular machine so interesting," Shirley said. "There are Pyxis machines all throughout the hospital. But the C-section recovery room isn't used all that often. There can be stretches of several hours when no one goes in there. Whoever broke into it must have known that. Choosing that machine to rob would dramatically reduce the chances of getting caught. And if they were quick..." She let her voice trail off.

"Here's what I don't get," Joy began. "You said the room door was open when you walked past, Anne?"

Anne nodded.

"Why did the person who broke in leave the door open?" Joy continued. "If you were going to break into a machine, why leave the door open while you did it?"

"Maybe they didn't," Anne said. "It's possible the door was closed while they were jimmying the drawers open, and they just left the door ajar when they went out."

"I think I can explain that," Shirley said. "That door doesn't stay closed. One of the hinges doesn't work right, and you have to wedge it. So this person may or may not have wanted the door closed, but it would have taken a lot of effort—and someone very familiar with the door—to get it to stay closed."

"Which means it may be someone who isn't especially familiar with the recovery room," Evelyn said.

"It might." Shirley shrugged. "Or it could just be someone who was in a hurry."

"Is there a security camera in there?" Joy asked.

"There's one in the hallway but not in the recovery room itself." Shirley took another sip of her coffee.

"Hopefully the security camera footage will show who did it. I'm sure the police are already looking into it."

"Let's hope they find the person who did this right away," Joy said. "That medicine... If it's not used right, it could be very dangerous. Even deadly."

"It's also expensive," Evelyn added. "I don't know exactly how much it's worth, but I imagine the hospital has a huge incentive to find out who took it."

"I think the police believe I might have done it," Anne said.

"What?" Evelyn's eyes were wide.

"No way." Joy shook her head.

"I should rephrase that. I'm sure they're just looking into every possibility," Anne said. "And since I was in the room, I'm a possibility."

"But they have to know you would never do such a thing," Evelyn said.

"And it doesn't make any sense," Shirley said. "You came and told me as soon as you discovered it. Why would you do that if you'd broken into the machine yourself?"

"*We* know you didn't do it," said Joy. "And the police will see that soon, if they haven't already."

"I'm sure they'll find the person soon enough," Anne said.

"Let's hope so." Shirley looked down at her phone. "I need to get back, I'm afraid."

"I should head back to work too," Evelyn said.

Anne said goodbye to her friends, but after they all left for their workstations, she sat at the table a little longer. She tried to get up, to make herself return to work, but whenever she thought about the fact that someone had wanted those opioids so badly they were willing to break into the machine to get them…well, that was a person who was desperate.

It made Anne unsettled in a way she hadn't been for quite a while.

Chapter Two

IT WAS JUST ANNE AND Ralph at the table for dinner that night. While Anne was grateful that Lili was home from deployment and was able to spend so much time with Addie, she missed having Addie's sunny presence around all the time. Their granddaughter had lived with them during Lili's overseas assignment, and Anne was still getting used to not having her at every meal. After Anne and Ralph had discussed his upcoming trip to the doctor and a funny video Addie had sent her, the topic of conversation turned to what had happened at the hospital that day.

"How is it that you manage to find yourself walking into mysteries so often?" Ralph asked, a smile on his face. He was slicing his pork chop into pieces with a sharp knife.

"I was literally just walking," Anne said. "I just happened to notice that the machine was open. Someone else would have discovered it sooner or later if it hadn't been me."

"Well, it was the talk of the hospital," Ralph said. Ralph had worked as a chaplain at Mercy since he'd retired from full-time ministry. "I heard the police were called in and they were interviewing everyone who was in the vicinity."

"That's true," Anne said. "I had to speak to a detective and tell him what I saw. He was asking questions like he thought I broke into the machine myself, even though I was the one who reported it. Why would I tell people about it if I was the one who did it?"

"I'm sure they're just dotting their i's and crossing their t's," Ralph said. "I'm sure they don't really believe you were responsible."

"The crazy thing is, whoever is responsible must work at the hospital." Anne took a bite and wiped her mouth with a stars and stripes paper napkin, left over from the Fourth last week.

"Why?" Ralph asked again. "It doesn't seem crazy to me. Statistically, healthcare professionals are just as likely to become addicted to painkillers as anyone else."

"I guess you're right." Anne thought for a moment, trying to understand what she really wanted to say. "You would just think, given how dangerous the drugs can be, that people at the hospital would know better."

"I'm sure they do know. That doesn't mean they wouldn't take them. I would imagine we're looking at a case of addiction here, and addiction doesn't care if you work at a hospital or not. There are stories all the time of doctors and nurses who steal from their workplaces to feed their addictions."

"I know." Addiction didn't discriminate. She wasn't sure what she was trying to say.

"Sure, in a world where people always behaved rationally, it would be unheard of," Ralph continued. "But the reality is, many healthcare professionals have easier access to addictive medications, and many of them struggle. You'd be surprised how many people working at every level of the healthcare system abuse opioids."

Anne nodded. He was right. It could be so frustrating that he was so reasonable sometimes.

"I guess I'm just surprised that someone who works at the hospital could be so far gone with addiction to do that," Anne tried again. "There were so many people around. They must have wanted those drugs really badly to risk it."

"That's true," Ralph said. "Though there is the possibility someone could have wanted the drugs for their value, instead of because they wanted them personally. Maybe someone knew where to sell them. They would be worth a hefty amount, no doubt, given the number that were taken."

"I thought of that," Anne said. "Do you think it's likely?"

Ralph waited a moment before shaking his head. "I think it's more likely we're looking at an individual facing addiction."

Then she had an idea. Ralph was a chaplain. That meant people told him things they wouldn't tell anyone else. She knew he wasn't supposed to share anything about his counseling, but... Well, she could ask, couldn't she? "Wait, you must know all about addiction among doctors and nurses because some of them talk to you, right?"

Ralph wiped his fingers on his napkin. "Even if they did, I wouldn't be able to tell you about it."

She sighed. "I know." Ralph had integrity—that was what made him such a good pastor and such a good man. He'd never betrayed a pastoral confidence to her in all the years they'd been married.

"In any case, there are plenty of people on that floor who aren't healthcare professionals, right?" Ralph said. "It could be any number of people, not just doctors and nurses."

"Yes." Anne thought about Olga, the housekeeper, and Luke, the transport, both of whom she'd seen just before she discovered the broken machine. "I suppose you're right, it could be someone who works there but isn't a medical professional."

"I don't know whether it's more likely or not," Ralph said. "And the last thing I want to do is cast suspicion on support staff. I'm just saying, addiction affects all kinds of people, across the spectrum. Even people you wouldn't expect."

He gave her a look, and she nodded, pushing back the anxiety that rose up in her at his words. She knew he was right.

"I'm sure this is making you think about—"

Anne didn't let him finish. "I know. Even people you would never expect."

Ralph watched her for moment. He looked like he was about to say something. She pressed her lips together and hoped he wouldn't. Finally, he seemed to make a decision.

"Whoever this person is, I think we should be praying for them," he said. Anne let out a breath. He was going to let it go. Thank goodness. "Someone must have been pretty desperate, and that means they need our compassion and our prayers."

Anne couldn't agree more.

After the dinner dishes were cleaned up, Ralph went to the living room to watch a baseball game, but Anne grabbed her laptop and a notebook and settled down at the kitchen table. It was already July, and she hadn't planned the vacation they were all taking in August yet. Lili hadn't been sure until last week whether she would be able to get the time off, and she was taking a business class at night to try to finish her degree. Now that they were all set on the first week of August, right before Addie went back to school, Anne had to get serious about planning.

Neither Ralph nor Lili had given her much to go on when she'd asked what they wanted to do for vacation, so she had decided a beach vacation would fit the bill. They could be in the water during the day and come home and cook simple meals at night and play games and relax. It sounded like heaven. There were plenty of beach towns just a short drive from Charleston, but Anne had heard so many good things about Isle of Palms, so she started there.

She pulled up a vacation rental website, typed in their dates, and found a long list of houses available to rent. She started at the top, with a house overlooking the beach with a beautiful blue pool and... oh wow. Well, that was a bit pricey. Anne looked down the list and ended up clicking past several pages of search results before she found some rentals that were in their price range. These houses weren't as nice; that was clear right away. There were no private pools, and the decor wasn't as updated, and they were farther from the beach.

Anne narrowed in on a condo that looked okay. The balcony had a water view, according to the photos. But she didn't really want a condo. She was hoping for a house, with a little more space to stretch out. She kept looking. Here was a cottage that looked adorable from the pictures. She clicked through and saw bright white shiplap and modern furniture. But the reviews were terrible. *"Owner is a crook."* *"Pictures are a lie." "Do not book."* Well then. *Moving on.* Anne found something listed as a villa—what did that even mean? It looked nice enough, but she soon saw that it only had one bedroom. Scratch that.

They would need at least two. There was nothing that seemed exactly right on this site. But that was okay. There were plenty of other beaches around here.

Next, Anne looked at rentals on Kiawah Island, but—wow, was there an extra zero on that price tag? There were some decent options on Sullivan's Beach and Folly's Beach but not as many as she'd hoped. She even looked farther north, at Myrtle Beach, and south to Tybee Island, but didn't find exactly what she was hoping for. Something peaceful, cute, clean, and cozy, and something that wouldn't break the bank. Had she waited too long? Were all the best houses gone by this point?

"I'm headed up to bed."

Anne jumped when Ralph spoke from the doorway.

"Goodness. Is it that time already?"

"It's past that time. The game went into extra innings."

She glanced up at the clock over the sink and saw that he was right.

"What are you so intent on in here anyway?" Ralph walked over and started massaging her shoulders, and Anne felt her muscles relax under his fingers.

"I'm trying to find the perfect beach house for our vacation."

"Ooh. That sounds nice. Any luck?"

"I've found plenty of places that look okay."

"That sounds promising."

"I'm hoping I can find something better than just okay."

Ralph leaned in and gave her a kiss on the cheek. "I'm sure you'll find something great. For now, though, how about bed?"

"I'll be up in a minute." She would just look at a few more places. "Maybe we shouldn't go to the beach. Would you spend some time thinking about where you might want to go?"

"Sure." And then, a moment later, he said, "We could always go to the mountains if the beach doesn't work out. I like the mountains, probably better than the beach."

They could do a mountain getaway. She was sure she could find a cute little cabin somewhere up in the hills, maybe the Blue Ridge Mountains or even the Smokies. Some place near hiking trails, a cabin with a place to build a fire for nights and views for days. That would be nice. She could just do a little poking around....

She heard Ralph head down the hallway and get ready for bed, but by the time she finally pushed herself up, bleary-eyed and frustrated, Ralph was already asleep. She just needed to do a little more research. She would find the perfect vacation rental soon.

Anne arrived at work Tuesday morning with questions turning through her mind. She hadn't slept well. Her mind kept drifting back to finding that open Pyxis machine. She'd gone over every detail of the sequence of events in her mind. Had Olga Dotov, from the cleaning crew, come from the recovery room, or was she just outside of it when Anne had seen her? Was Luke Merritt, the transport, coming from the room when she'd seen him? What about any of the nurses and doctors and patients on the floor? Which of them had broken into the machine, and why?

When Anne got to the volunteer room, she found that she wasn't the only one thinking about the theft. Aurora wasn't in the room, and as Anne put her purse in her locker and slipped on the sweater she often wore around the hospital, she overheard another volunteer named Polly saying, "It's an open secret that the pill count is often off. Someone is taking pills from the machines." Polly was eating a small bowl of instant oatmeal at the little table in the middle of the room. It smelled like apple cinnamon from here. "The administration knows that and is working to figure out who it is."

Anne wasn't trying to listen. She didn't want to hear gossip. She focused on slipping her cell phone into her pocket and straightening her sweater.

"You think?" Mandy, who often volunteered in the nursery, used the mirror over the sink to apply a coat of pink lipstick. "I don't know. I saw that new transport guy on the floor yesterday right around twelve thirty. That's when they're saying the machine was discovered, right?"

"That's what I heard." Polly stirred her oatmeal.

"Well, Luke was there around then. I know because I'd called down to get someone to move those wheelchairs that were clogging up the hallway, and he showed up just before my break. He's totally shady."

"He's definitely got some…unique qualities," Polly said.

Anne pulled her water bottle out of her purse and walked over to the water cooler to fill it. The other volunteers kept chatting as if she wasn't there.

"He's sketchy." Mandy pressed her lips together and checked them in the mirror. "Listen. You know that club Shade over on King?"

"I've heard of it." Polly took a bite of her oatmeal and then said, "It's not really my thing."

"I would never go there either, ew. That place is so gross. But my brother used to work there, as a security guard. He told me some stories that would make your skin crawl."

"Didn't the police raid that place?"

"Yeah, like every other week." Mandy straightened up and twisted her lipstick back into the tube. "That's my point. There are so many drugs flowing through there. It wouldn't be hard to find a buyer for the pills that were taken yesterday."

"You think someone took them so they could sell them at the club?" Polly asked dubiously.

"I mean, why not? They're worth a lot, right? Isn't that why the police are involved?"

Anne's water bottle was filled to the top, and she stepped back and took a sip to lower the level before she screwed the lid back on.

"I guess." Polly seemed to be considering the idea. "But how does that make you think it was Luke?"

"Luke used to work at Shade. In security, with my brother. That's what I'm trying to tell you. Who else could it have been? He's strong enough to break into the machine, and he has a way to sell them through the club. I think he's the one who took them. In fact, maybe that's the reason he started working here in the first place, to get better access to drugs so he could sell them."

"I suppose that's one idea," Polly said.

"You still think it's the nurse?" Mandy asked, and Polly nodded.

Anne moved toward her locker and set the water bottle back inside.

"What do you think, Anne?"

Anne turned and saw that both women were looking at her. In that moment, she felt a rush of emotions—put on the spot, for sure, but also frustration with herself for having listened to the gossip in the first place. But she also felt curiosity. Could what they said be true?

"I don't know," Anne said honestly. "But I think it's time for me to be heading out." She certainly didn't need to contribute to their chatter.

"Aren't you gonna wait for Aurora to tell us where to go?" Polly cocked her head.

"I think I'm just going to start off at the gift shop and see if there are any flowers that need to be delivered." She closed her locker and spun the dial to lock it, and then she waved and smiled at Polly and Mandy before she headed out.

Anne wasn't in the mood to wait for the infernally slow elevators, so she took the stairs down to the first level, thinking through what she'd heard. It was all hearsay. Gossip. But was there any truth in it? Any chance that Luke was selling painkillers through the club where he used to work? Her footsteps echoed in the cement stairwell. She supposed it was possible. But there was also that unknown nurse who was suspected of skimming pills from the machine. And there was also Olga, as well as lots of other people known to be on the floor at the time of the theft.

Anne pushed open the door to the lobby and stepped out into the hallway. This hall, which led from the lobby to the rear of the hospital, overlooking Charleston Harbor, was one the main arteries of the building, and dozens of people walked past. She smiled at a couple of residents she'd met, their white coats swishing an ER nurse, and a group of older women wearing visitor badges. And then—well, how lucky was this?

"Olga!"

The housekeeper pushed her cart toward the service elevators, her head down. She looked up at Anne, and Anne waved. Anne didn't know Olga well, but she had chatted with her once or twice. Anne chatted with everyone.

"Hello, Anne." Olga's curly dark hair was pulled back into a ponytail, and she wore the light blue smock of the maintenance crew. She stopped pushing her cart and smiled. "How are you?"

"I'm doing okay." This was her chance. Normally, she would start with some pleasantries, play up the Southern charm, but Olga was on duty and wouldn't have a lot of time to chat. "Did you hear about the theft yesterday from the C-section recovery room?"

"Yes, I did. It was very disturbing." Olga had a faint Eastern European accent. She'd once told Anne she was born in Bulgaria. "I was very sorry to hear of it."

"I was there on the floor when it was discovered," Anne said. "I was delivering flowers to a couple who'd just had a baby. A beautiful little girl. I didn't see or hear anything, unfortunately, but I sure wish I had."

Olga nodded but didn't speak.

"Hang on. You were there too, right?" Anne tried to make it sound as though the thought had just occurred to her. "I remember seeing you on the ward. Did you notice anything? I keep thinking, someone had to see something, there has to be a way to figure out what happened."

"No," Olga said. "I'm often in the labor and delivery ward, but I wasn't on that floor at the time."

Wait. What? Olga had been there. Anne had seen her with her own eyes. Hadn't she?

"Really?" Anne tried to keep skepticism from her voice. "I could have sworn I saw you around."

"No." Olga shook her head and then gestured at her cart. "I'm sorry. I have to go." And without another word, she moved away. Anne stood still for a moment, watching her go. Was she crazy? Or was Olga lying to her? She was sure she'd seen Olga with her supplies right by the door to the recovery room. Why would she lie about that?

There was only one reason Anne could think of.

She realized she was blocking the hallway when she saw that a woman with a guide dog had to swerve to get around her. She turned and made her way to the gift shop, still puzzling over the interaction with Olga.

# Chapter Three

THE SMELL OF COFFEE HIT Anne as she made her way into the gift shop. Joy had somehow made the space feel warm and welcoming, even in the lobby of this modern wing of the hospital.

"Good morning." Joy was tidying the rack of greeting cards, and she straightened up when Anne walked in. "How are you today?"

"Just fine." Anne felt more peaceful simply being here with her friend. "I was checking to see if you had any flower deliveries ready to go."

"Not so far." Joy cocked her head. "You look tired. How about some coffee?"

Now that she mentioned it, coffee sounded wonderful. "Yes, please."

"Come on back here, and we'll get you fixed up." Joy gestured for Anne to follow her to the little break room at the back of the gift shop. "I bet you couldn't sleep because you were worried about that theft."

"I just couldn't get my mind to settle," Anne said.

"Of course you couldn't." Joy poured coffee from the pot she always had brewing into a paper cup. She added cream and sugar without even having to ask and then handed the cup to Anne. "You feel responsible because you found it, don't you?"

"In a weird way, I guess I do," Anne admitted. "The hospital and the police are both looking into it, but I don't know. I can't help feeling that I must have seen something or know some detail that can help."

"You always do love a mystery," Joy said.

Anne laughed. It was true that she and her friends had put together the pieces on some puzzling mysteries over the past year. "Look who's talking."

"Well, I'm sure that if there's anything we can do to help, the hospital will let us know," Joy said. She gestured toward the table, and they both sat down.

Anne nodded. And yet… She was a suspect, it seemed. And that didn't sit well with her. If she could find out who had actually taken the pills, that would clear her name.

"What do you know about Luke Merritt?" Anne asked, before taking a sip of her coffee.

Joy cocked her head. "Why do I know that name?"

"I mentioned him yesterday. He was on the floor at the right time."

"Ah. I don't know him at all, I'm afraid."

"Have you ever met Olga Dotov?" Anne wasn't sure what she was hoping for, but she felt like she had to ask.

"I don't know her well, but she goes to my church."

"She does?" Joy went to a nondenominational church that met in an old building they'd bought from a Methodist congregation.

"I've seen her at services a few times. She usually attends Saturday evening, which is more geared toward families. But I've seen her on Sunday mornings. We've said hello and chatted at coffee hour a bit. She's got a little boy, oh, maybe ten or so. Cute kid."

"What do you think of her?"

Joy pressed her lips together. "She seems great."

"What?" Anne narrowed her eyes.

"What?"

"There was more there. Something you didn't want to tell me."

"No there wasn't."

"Joy Atkins, you're a terrible liar."

Joy waited a moment before she said, "I don't know if I should say anything."

"Is what you know about her relevant to what happened here yesterday?"

Joy sighed. "Look, it doesn't mean anything, necessarily. Right? But Olga shared her testimony at church last year. She actually started coming to our church through the NA meetings that happen there every week."

"Narcotics Anonymous." Anne was very familiar with the organization. They'd helped her brother—for a time, at least.

"In her testimony, she said she started taking painkillers after her son's father left, and she got hooked. She ended up losing her job. Losing custody of her kid—it was bad."

"That's awful."

"But losing her son was a wake-up call. She got help, worked hard at getting and staying clean, and ended up at the meetings at our church. Through those, she started attending services, and she came to faith. In her testimony, she talked about how her relationship with

Christ had changed her life and how hard she'd fought to get her son back."

"That's a beautiful story. She must be a strong person."

"No doubt about that. Also, let's not discount the awesome power of Christ's saving grace."

"Amen."

"I worry that she's going to be accused because of her history, though," Joy said.

"We certainly don't want the wrong person getting blamed," Anne said. "Though I suppose there's always the chance she's using again."

"Ugh. I sure hope not," Joy said, cringing.

"I hope not too. Addiction is so hard," Anne said. People relapsed all the time, even after they got clean. Her brother Nick was exhibit A. Sometimes people slipped back into using, no matter how hard they tried. "Let's hope she's been able to stay clean. But I just had a weird interaction with her."

"You saw her?"

"I ran into her in the hallway just a minute ago. I mentioned I'd seen her on the floor around the time of the theft—"

"You accused her of stealing the medicine?"

"No, I didn't accuse her," Anne said, shaking her head. "I mentioned I was there too and wondered if she'd seen anything. And she totally clammed up. She said she hadn't been there at all."

"But you saw her, didn't you?"

"I did. I'm sure it was her." Anne took another sip of the coffee. "So why would she say she wasn't there?"

"I mean, I could see why she'd be a bit squirrely, if she thought you were saying she might have taken that medicine," Joy said. "Given her history and all. But it doesn't make sense that she would lie about being there."

"So why would she?" Anne asked. "Is it because she is nervous about people accusing her? Or is there another reason? Is it because she doesn't want people to know she was there because she did take the medicine?"

Joy sat back in her chair. She crossed her arms over her chest and tilted her chin up. "There has to be a way to prove that she was there. Or that you were mistaken. One way or the other, there's got to be record of it. What about security camera footage?"

"Shirley did say there was a camera in the hallway outside of the recovery room."

"I'm sure the police and hospital security are looking into it," Joy said. "But it sure would be nice to take a look at the footage. Then you'd know for sure whether she was there and she's lying, or whether you're crazy."

"Hey!"

"Fine. Whether you were mistaken." Joy picked up her cup and looked down at the coffee. "Why don't you just ask the security team if you could see the footage?" Joy was already pushing herself up. "Here. I'll make another cup of coffee. You can take it to Norm. See if he can get you a copy of that footage."

"I suppose it can't hurt to ask." Norm Ashford worked the night shift, and by early morning he was usually grateful for a cup of coffee.

Anne finished her own coffee, thanked Joy, and, a few minutes later, was walking toward the security team office, which was tucked into an out-of-the-way alcove off the main lobby. She knocked gently on the door, and, when she heard someone inside yell for her to enter, she stepped into the room.

"Hi Anne." It wasn't Norm Ashford in today, but Steven Phillips. Anne knew Steven. He'd had something of a crush on Shirley a little while ago, which had helped Shirley recognize her feelings for Garrison Baker, one of the hospital administrators. The two had become an item in the last few months, and her hospital friends couldn't be more pleased with the match. "How are you?"

"I'm doing well. Yourself?"

Steven was seated in one of the chairs in front of a series of monitors, each showing nearly a dozen security camera feeds. "Things are all right. Can't complain." He eyed the cup in her hand.

"Would you like some coffee?"

Steven laughed. "I'm not gonna lie, that would be most welcome. But what's the catch?"

"There's no catch." She held it out. "Though I was hoping I could ask for some information about what happened yesterday."

"Ah yes. You were part of the excitement, weren't you?"

"I suppose you could call it that. It was so disturbing to see the machine forced open like that." Anne couldn't get the image out of her head. "I'm really hoping that whoever did this is found."

"We're working on it," Steven said. "We have security camera footage from the hallway outside the room, and we've narrowed it down to about an hour-long window when the theft could have happened, so we're talking to everyone who went in and out of the room in that time. Including, I might add, you."

Anne's fingers tightened around the coffee cup.

"Now, don't worry. No one really suspects that you did it. But you were in the room for nearly a minute, which the police seem to think is long enough to have broken into the machine."

"A minute? There's no way I was in there that long." She was in the room for fifteen seconds, max.

"The footage shows it was almost a minute." Steven shrugged.

How was that possible? She'd gone in, noticed the machine, and headed back out. Was she really that far off in her estimation?

"I'd like to see that security camera footage," Anne said. "That's actually what I came in here to ask about."

"Huh." Steven studied her. "Well, I don't see any harm in it, personally, but I would need to run that request past Seamus to see what he says." Seamus McCord was the head of security. "As you would imagine, this is all being dealt with at the highest levels."

"I would imagine," she said. "But if it's possible, I sure would like to see it." When she came in here, she'd mostly wanted to check if Olga appeared in the footage, but now she also wanted to find out if Steven was right about her being in it for almost a minute.

"Maybe you and your friends could help figure out who did this. You all have done that before, haven't you?" He said it with a laugh, and Anne tried not to feel dismissed.

"We have. And you never know." She smiled, not sure what else to do.

"Well, I can't give you a copy of the footage right now, but I can promise I will forward the request to Seamus and let you know." He looked up at her. "You want to give me your cell number? I can text you when I get an answer from him."

"That would be great."

Anne walked out of the office and decided she should probably head up to the volunteer room to see if Aurora was back and find out what she wanted her to do. She took the stairs. Mandy and Polly were gone when she arrived, but Aurora was there, looking at something on a computer screen.

"There you are."

"Good morning. You weren't here when I got in, so I went down to the gift shop to see if there were any deliveries."

Aurora nodded, though Anne couldn't tell if she was satisfied by the explanation. Aurora did things by the book and didn't love it when her volunteers went rogue.

"I have you down for discharge duty this morning. There are a couple of patients on two waiting to be taken down."

"I'm on it." Discharge duty was one of Anne's favorite volunteer activities. She loved helping people leave the hospital. As much as she enjoyed being here, most patients were only too glad to be released, and she was happy to help them be on their way. She spent the next hour happily chatting with patients as she wheeled them to the big silver elevators and out the rear entrance, with its view over Charleston Harbor. But after she'd helped several patients, there was a lull, and Anne considered what to do. She hadn't gotten a text from Steven yet, so she couldn't see the security camera footage. She couldn't eliminate or dig deeper into Olga's story until she knew whether she was lying. Her mind drifted back to the conversation about Luke Merritt. Was he supplying drugs to the club where he used to work, or was that just vicious gossip? Anne didn't know. She bit her lip.

But those weren't the only suspects. There was also the nurse who was potentially taking medicine from the Pyxis machines, whoever she was. Anne knew several of the nurses on the Labor and Delivery floor, but not all of them. Did any of the ones she knew seem like they would be abusing opioids?

But that was a ridiculous question. Addiction wasn't usually obvious. It could be anyone, and she would probably never know.

Still, Evelyn and Shirley had both heard that the hospital was looking into whether someone had been taking medicine. Was there a way to figure out who it was? If she could find out whether someone really had been stealing medication, that would identify another suspect for the theft yesterday. And, well, if it also took suspicion off Anne in the meantime, so much the better. She thought for a moment and then decided to make a trip downstairs to see Evelyn. Anne headed back to the first floor and made her way to the records room, which was near the entrance to the emergency room. She opened the door and stepped inside, where she was greeted by Pam, one of the full-time employees who kept the place running.

"Hi there, Anne." Stacia looked up from her computer. Stacia was young, but she was very detail oriented and was great at keeping Evelyn organized. "Looking for Evelyn?"

Anne didn't really have much reason to come into this part of the hospital unless she was looking for her friend. "Yes. Do you know if she's around?"

"She's in the Vault."

Anne should have guessed. Evelyn loved nothing more than poking around in the dusty, windowless room that held the hospital's oldest records, some going back hundreds of years.

"I'll go see if I can pull her away."

Anne walked through the modern records room and through the door that led to the Vault, where she found Evelyn hunched over a sheaf of tea-colored paper.

"What did you find?"

"I found this stack of letters tucked onto a shelf at the back." She gestured toward a large safe. "They're from the Civil War."

"What?"

"I knew Mercy Hospital treated soldiers throughout the war. We have plenty of records of that. But I haven't seen anything like this. Here's a stash of letters from a soldier after the battle of Fort Sumter."

"He was injured in the battle?" Every Charleston native knew about the battle that had begun the Civil War.

"He was. Shot in the leg. From the later letters, it appears he went on to lose the leg but not before the gangrene had spread."

"That doesn't sound good."

"It wasn't. Three of the letters are to his wife and young son. Two of them are to his mother. The last letter in the stack is from a nurse who treated him throughout his stay, informing his family that he passed peacefully in his sleep." She held out the final letter, which was written in swirling, looping script with a very fine nib. "This nurse, Millie Sullivan, actually seems to have written all the letters in the stack for him. Joshua Palmer, from Harrisburg, Pennsylvania."

"So he was a Yankee?"

"He was indeed. And the nurses here took care of him all the same."

Anne nodded. Mercy Hospital, like most medical facilities in both the North and the South, treated soldiers from both armies. The doctors and nurses here cared about saving lives, not about politics.

"Why did Millie write the letters for him?" Anne asked.

"They don't say." Evelyn looked down at the pages and then back up again. "It's possible that he wasn't literate—that wasn't all that uncommon. But my guess is he was in too much pain to do it himself. The letters make a lot of references to how much pain he's in."

"Goodness. I thought soldiers were supposed to write home about how great things were, even when it wasn't true. Make sure their mothers didn't worry and all that."

"I don't suppose there's any rule for how a man dying far from his family in enemy territory should act," Evelyn said.

"I suppose you're right," Anne said. "Why was he in so much pain? Wasn't there enough medicine to help him?"

"Goodness, no," Evelyn said. "Especially that early in the war. Both sides were completely unprepared for the bloodbath the war would become, and far more soldiers died because of infection and disease than on the battlefield. Medical supplies of any kind were limited, and the little chloroform and laudanum and ether they did have was reserved for the worst cases or for the surgeries themselves. There wasn't much to spare for the patients as they recuperated."

"How awful." Even with the dangers inherent in today's highly addictive painkillers, Anne was grateful for the relief they provided patients. She couldn't imagine the suffering that must have gone on at the hospital without adequate supplies.

"The letters are fascinating, though. Joshua asks about his little sisters and tells his mother not to worry about him."

"She worried about him every minute of every day, regardless." As the mother of a soldier herself, Anne knew this for a fact.

"No doubt. He also asks his wife about her vegetable garden and whether their son is talking yet."

Anne felt a pang of sympathy. She knew how hard it was on Lili to have missed so many milestones in Addie's life while she was deployed abroad. And video chat and text messages made it easier for Addie to keep in touch with Lili while she was gone. Joshua would have only had letters—which, as they saw, sometimes never made it to their intended destination.

"He describes life at Fort Sumter prior to the attack, and his letters give a really good glimpse into what it was like in the hospital during the war."

"And how was it?"

"Awful. I've already told you there was no pain relief and high mortality rates. But it was still better than a field hospital, where there were too few doctors and nurses and supplies and zero infrastructure. At least if a patient made it from the field hospital to here, they had a fighting chance."

"But not poor Joshua."

"Sadly, not him."

Anne thought for a moment. "But wait. If Millie wrote these letters for him, why are they still here? Why weren't they mailed to Pennsylvania?"

Pain Relief

"That's what I can't figure out," Evelyn said. "They should have been sent out as they were written, but the whole group of letters—six in all, written over the course of nearly a month—were here stuffed into the Vault all this time."

"So his family never got them," Anne said.

"Apparently not. Mail was unreliable at this time, especially once Charleston was a war zone, so maybe she was holding on to them until she could be sure they would make it." Evelyn shrugged.

"Or maybe she decided not to mail them after all," Anne suggested. "Maybe she worried that all the talk about how much pain he was in would bother his family too much."

"I doubt that's it," Evelyn said. "I mean, I hope she didn't take it upon herself to decide what news was worthy of passing along. But given how dedicated to him she was, taking the time to transcribe his letters like this with so many other patients to care for, I get the impression she was a caring woman who really just wanted the best for Joshua."

"That fits with what I know of the nurses at Mercy today," Anne said. "But if the letters were never mailed, do you think the family ever found out what happened to Joshua?"

"I don't know," Evelyn said. "That's what I was wondering too. I imagine they must have gotten some sort of official communication from the army about his death. But there were probably not many details, if any. Most of the communications I've seen have been simple telegrams. 'Your son killed at Gettysburg, deep condolences,' that kind of thing."

"That makes it all the more tragic that these didn't get mailed," Anne said. "If his family never found out how he died or that he survived a month beyond the battle—that's awful. Or never knew someone cared for him here at Mercy and did her best to keep him comfortable, despite the circumstances."

"I was thinking the same thing. And I was wondering."

"Wondering what?"

"Well, his mother and father are long gone by now, obviously. His wife and son too. But I wondered if I could get these letters to the family anyway. That maybe they would like to have the letters, even though all the people who would have known Joshua are several generations back."

"I imagine they would," Anne said. "If long-lost letters written by one of my ancestors were found, I would love to see those. Especially if they addressed questions my family had never known the answers to."

"That's what I was thinking too."

"You're going to try to find them, aren't you?"

"I was thinking I might do some digging, just to see if I could locate his people," Evelyn said.

"That sounds great. Please let me know what you find."

"I will. But anyway. That's not what you came in here for. What's going on?" Evelyn set the stack of letters to the side and turned back to face Anne.

"I've been thinking about that medication theft," Anne said.

"I had a feeling that was it." Evelyn gently set the letters aside and gestured for Anne to sit down in the rickety folding chair next to her.

Anne settled gently into the chair and said, "Yesterday, you mentioned Pyxis records that were inaccurate."

"It's something the administration has been watching," Evelyn said. "Just last week they asked me for records from all the Pyxis machines on the labor and delivery ward."

"And they have someone reading through the records, looking for patterns? To see if they can figure out who is causing the pill count to be off?"

"That's what I assume, although I don't know who it is."

"Would it be possible for me to get a copy of the records?" Anne asked.

Instead of answering, Evelyn leaned back in her chair and studied Anne.

"This has really gotten to you, hasn't it?" Evelyn asked.

"It has," Anne admitted. "They seem to think I could have done it. I need to prove that it wasn't me."

Evelyn watched her for another moment before she continued. "It's more than that, though, I think. You're always curious about mysteries, but this is more than that. This is personal, isn't it?"

Anne nodded. Was she ready to talk about this? She wasn't sure she could tell Evelyn why this meant so much to her without falling apart. Would Evelyn judge her for her role in it all? For not doing more?

But Evelyn was one of her dearest friends. If Anne couldn't share this kind of thing with her, who could she tell?

"It's my brother," Anne said. "Nick."

"You have a brother?"

"I do."

"I've never heard you mention him."

"I—we're not close. Not anymore."

Evelyn waited, gesturing for her to go on.

"He lives in Atlanta. He was always athletic, good-looking smart, popular. The golden boy. He married the head cheerleader, had two kids. They're both in college now. He was a developer. He bought land, built houses, sold them, that kind of thing."

"You keep using the past tense."

Anne nodded. "Right. He had a great life. But then, ten years ago, he had an accident at work. He was inspecting the roof of one of the homes his firm built, and he fell. He was lucky to live, to be honest, but he ended up breaking several bones in his back. He was on bed rest for nearly six weeks. And he was in a lot of pain."

"Oh dear."

"Yep. So his doctor prescribed oxycodone to help with the pain. This was back in the days when doctors were prescribing that stuff right and left. The drug companies were really pushing it, making money hand over fist. I know they're a lot more careful with it now—"

"Several multibillion-dollar lawsuits later," Evelyn said, shaking her head.

"Well, he got hooked. Once he ran out of refills, he went to another doctor. And then another. There was no shortage of doctors willing to write him a prescription. And then, when those ran out, he started turning to...less legal methods of obtaining the drugs."

"I imagine the rest of his life wasn't going so well by this point," Evelyn said.

"You can say that again," Anne said. "His addiction was already destroying his business. Unbeknownst to anyone else, he drained his bank accounts to get his hands on more pills, and soon was funneling money from his company into his personal accounts to cover his tracks. Pretty soon the business imploded, and so did his marriage."

"Oh, Anne. I'm so sorry."

"By that point, he was in so deep he couldn't even see the possibility of a way out. He was in and out of rehab for several years. He would get clean for a while, but then he would relapse. We tried to help and lent him money several times. We paid his security deposit for an apartment when he had nowhere else to go. We paid for his treatment a couple of times. And we were glad to do it. At least until we realized it wasn't helping."

"So what happened?"

"We stopped helping him. We had to. It wasn't just that he never even attempted to pay us back. It was because after the third time we gave him money for treatment, we found out he'd spent it on heroin instead."

"Oh no."

"That's when we cut him off. We lost touch with him for a while. I think he was on the streets for a bit, though that was never confirmed. His wife divorced him, and his children wanted nothing to do with him. We've been in touch a few times over the past few years, but it's just so hard. He was clean for a while, a few years back. We were so proud of him and started seeing him more. He got a job, and it looked like he was trying to get his life back on track. But then he relapsed. After a while, it was just too hard. Every time he relapsed, we'd get our hearts broken all over again. And the lies were the worst. We just couldn't know when he was telling us the truth or whether it was the drugs talking. So we—well, we don't really have much contact with him these days."

"That sounds awful, Anne." And then she added, "Thank you for telling me."

Anne nodded but didn't say anything for a moment. Then, finally, she said, "I guess that's why this whole thing has bothered me so much. It feels like…well, it's bringing it all back up again. With Nick."

"I can understand why," Evelyn said.

"I didn't comprehend, before, how easy it is to slip into addiction. How it happens to people you would never expect. How hard it is to recognize. Even when he was in the throes of a full-blown addiction, we didn't see it. He was successful, handsome, charming—we just didn't see how someone like him could throw it all away for some pills. It took a long time for us to understand that he was so desperate he didn't feel like he had a choice. He was already in way too deep for anything else to matter."

"Do you think that if you can find out who took those drugs, you'll be able to help them?" Evelyn asked gently. *The way you weren't able to help Nick,* was the part Evelyn left unsaid, but Anne understood.

Was that it? Anne hadn't thought of it that way, but now that Evelyn had said the words, it did kind of fit.

"I guess that's part of it," Anne said.

"I see." Compassion wreathed Evelyn's face. "And I would help you if I could. Please believe me when I tell you I would give you whatever you want it were up to me." She sat back and sighed.

"But I'm afraid I can't give you the Pyxis records. I'm bound by a confidentiality clause in my contract, so I can't just hand out information that relates to personnel files. Unless you're asking in an official capacity, my options are few."

Anne sighed. She'd had a feeling that was what Evelyn would say.

"To be honest, I'm not sure how much it would help you, if at all really," Evelyn said. "When I printed the records for the L&D ward machines out for the last few weeks for Garrison, they filled a three-ring binder. The really thick kind. And the pages are all tiny type and very hard to make sense of in any case. You need to know the nurses' ID numbers and the code numbers for all the different medications to make sense of them."

It sounded daunting, but Anne figured that there would be a way to make sense of all that if she could get her hands on the records. But she understood why Evelyn couldn't just hand them to her.

"I'm sorry I can't help you with that. But if you want to learn any more about how they treated patients here during the Civil War, do I have some reading for you."

"I'll keep that in mind."

"Thank you for sharing with me," Evelyn said again, and Anne pushed herself up. Evelyn stood too, and pulled her into a hug. Anne embraced her friend, and then she stepped away, said goodbye, and headed back out into the main records room. She waved at Stacia, and then, once she was in the lobby again, she pulled out her phone to check the time and saw that she had received a text while she was talking to Evelyn. She squinted at the screen and read the message, and then she reread it.

Then she laughed and turned around and headed back into the records room. She walked straight to the Vault this time. Evelyn was studying the letters, and her eyes widened when she saw Anne standing in front of her again.

"You said you couldn't show me the records unless I was asking in an official capacity," Anne said. "Well, now I am. I just got a message that Garrison is going to let me have the security camera footage. I'm going to ask him if I can get a copy of those records too."

Chapter Four

A FEW MINUTES LATER, ANNE settled in Garrison Baker's office on the fifth floor. Garrison was seated behind his desk, and Anne sat across from him, facing the wall of historic maps and drawings of plans for the hospital.

"So I hear you've been asking about the drug theft that happened yesterday on the L&D floor," Garrison said. He was one of the top administrators at the hospital, and though he had a reputation as a no-nonsense businessman, Anne knew that he was a kind, thoughtful man. He and Shirley had been getting to know one another better in recent months, and Anne couldn't help but think they might have a future together.

"Just a bit," Anne said. "I was the one who found the machine broken into, so I'm anxious to see whoever did it caught." She didn't mention that she believed she was also a suspect. Surely he knew that already.

Garrison pressed his hands together, his elbows resting on his desk.

"The thing is, we're anxious to catch the person too," Garrison said. "Did you see the newspaper this morning?"

Anne shook her head. She didn't have time to read the paper as regularly as she wished. Garrison held up the *Charleston Times* and showed her the front page. DRUG THEFT AT MERCY HOSPITAL LEAVES STAFF STUMPED, the headline read.

"Yikes," Anne said.

"It doesn't look great for the hospital," Garrison said. "Never mind the value of the medication that was stolen."

"And the fact that it means someone on staff may be suffering from a serious addiction," Anne said. "To be that desperate."

Garrison didn't respond, and then a moment later he said, "Right. Of course."

"If the person can be found, hopefully they can get the help they must need."

"Exactly," he agreed. "We want to give our team the help they need. And the police are investigating, of course. We've given them all the information and leads we have. But I heard you were asking questions, and I started to wonder. You and your friends have found the solutions to a few tricky problems we've had around here in the past year."

"We've just been able to ask the right questions."

"Under normal circumstances, we would deny your request for security camera footage, since this is a police matter," he said. Her request had clearly gone through Seamus all the way to Garrison. "But after I thought about it some, I realized that more eyes may be better, in this case."

"Thank you," Anne said.

"I'll make sure you get a copy of the footage," he promised. "But here's the thing. I need to ask that you handle this discreetly, because it *is* a police matter."

So that was why he'd called her to his office. To tell her to keep it quiet that he was giving her access to the footage. Well, she could do that. "Of course," Anne said.

"And if you discover anything important, you'll need to turn it over to the hospital and the police right away," he continued.

"Could I also get a copy of the Pyxis machine records from the floor? I wanted to look at those as well."

He thought for a moment. "Why do you want those?"

"I know that there have been discrepancies in the pill count. I was thinking that if someone has been taking medication from the machines, they would likely be a primary suspect here."

Garrison waited a moment, and seemed to weigh his words carefully. "The police are looking into that angle as well."

"But I might see something they don't."

Again, there was a pause before he said, "I'll ask to have a copy of those records released to you as well. Again, though, on strictest confidentiality. The hospital is also looking through the records, but if you see something we miss, we'd be glad to hear it."

"Of course." Anne sat back and thought. She should let Garrison return to work. But this was her chance to ask any questions about the break-in.

"Have the police narrowed down the list of suspects?"

"I don't know. I'm not privy to their investigation." He folded his hands. "I hope that if you find anything, you will be a little more forthcoming."

"If I find anything, I'll share it with you," Anne said. "Have they figured out how he—or she, I guess—got the machine open? They must have used a tool of some kind."

"Funny you should mention that," Garrison said. "I just got word about that. Sterile Processing reported a C-section kit had gone missing yesterday."

Sterile Processing was the department that collected and sterilized used equipment from around the hospital and packaged the clean equipment for use with patients. "That's the pack of tools that gets brought into the operating room?" Anne had seen those before. They were sterilized packages of equipment containing whatever tools might be needed in the operating room. Nurses set them in place before the patient and the doctor came in. She imagined a C-section kit contained scalpels, clamps, and a needle and thread for after the surgery, among other things.

"That's right. Our inventory management team keeps track of what equipment is used and when it makes it back to Sterilization"— that was the room with the machines that cleaned and sterilized all medical equipment before it was sent out to be reused—"and last night they noticed that a C-section kit had gone missing."

"You mean one more kit was taken than C-sections performed?"

"Exactly."

Goodness. They really did track every single thing in this hospital. She supposed it was good management to know where your equipment was and to make sure you knew when it was used and returned, but she couldn't imagine the number of hours that would take.

"It turns out a ribbon retractor was found in the trash can next to the machine yesterday afternoon. It appears to be from the missing kit."

"A ribbon retractor?" What in the world was that?

"Like this." He reached behind him and picked up a long, thin piece of metal. It was roughly the shape of an emery board, but longer, and made of silver metal. "Used for pulling back tissue."

Thankfully, he didn't say more about that. She studied it and saw that it was thin enough to wedge into the top of the drawer and strong enough to pry it open.

"Is that the one that was used?"

"No. The police have that one, to search for fingerprints. This is another one that I showed the other administrators."

She nodded. "So it seems like whoever broke into the machine has at least some knowledge of medical equipment."

"I think that's safe to say. However, this is a hospital, so I think it's reasonable to assume most of the staff at the hospital have some knowledge of medical equipment."

It was a fair point. It wouldn't be hard for anyone—from cleaning crew to the highest paid surgeon—to know what basic medical equipment was and where it was kept. But the thief didn't just have the knowledge. He or she had access too.

"Where are the C-section kits stored?" Anne asked.

"In the surgical supply closet," Garrison said. "Everyone who removes something from the closet is required to sign it out."

So the medical supplies weren't as tightly controlled as the medication itself, though that made sense.

"But whoever did take it didn't sign it out?" she asked.

"Right."

"Who has access to the surgical supply closet?"

Garrison shrugged. "You have to punch in a code to open the door, but I suppose it wouldn't be that hard to discover the password."

"So it pretty much could have been anyone," Anne said, and he nodded.

"Unfortunately, yes. Anyone who knew they were there and learned the code."

Anne thought this through. This pointed to the thief being someone who didn't have access to the Pyxis machines—so, not a nurse—but who had spent enough time in the hospital that they knew where the supplies were kept and how to recognize and find a tool that could be used to pry open the machine. Either Luke the transport or Olga the cleaner would fit that bill.

Then she had a thought. "Do you know who found the ribbon retractor in the garbage?"

"One of the cleaning staff," he said.

"Do you know who it was?" Anne asked.

"I don't." He narrowed his eyes. "Why?"

Anne thought it was probably best not to voice her idea just yet. "It might be important," she said.

He was quiet for a moment, and then he said, "Again, I need to ask you to please be discreet about this. The footage and the records…"

"No one will know," Anne said. "I understand."

"All right then." Garrison nodded, and Anne pushed herself up to go. He turned back to his computer screen, and she made her way downstairs to the records room once again. When she got there, Evelyn had a thick binder on her desk.

"Garrison emailed me to say you could have these," she said, and she handed the binder to Anne. "Some light reading."

"I'll dig in as soon as I can," Anne said.

She tucked the binder under her arm and headed to Security, where Stephen was waiting with a thumb drive.

"Seamus gave the okay," he said, handing it to her. "I hope you see something we've missed."

"I hope so too," she said.

"I've given you the window of time the police are focusing on, plus a little extra on either side. The last patient was removed from the recovery room at eleven thirty, and you discovered the machine open just after twelve thirty. So there's about an hour of video here. Let me know if you need any more."

"Will do."

She took both the binder and the thumb drive back to the volunteer room to tuck them into her locker, and she found Aurora waiting for her.

"Oh, there you are, Anne," she said. "Peggy is about to go on break at noon. Could you cover the front desk for a bit?"

"Sure thing."

"Great," Aurora said.

Anne pulled her phone out of her pocket and glanced at the screen as she stepped into the hallway. It was 11:51. That gave her a few minutes until she needed to relieve Peggy. Just enough time to make one more stop. Instead of heading down the stairs, she walked along the second-floor hallway into the historic wing and followed the winding corridors until she reached the transport office. Many people didn't realize how important the transport team was in moving patients and equipment throughout the hospital, but without this department, they would be stuck.

"Hi there." Anne stepped through the doorway to the little room, not unlike the volunteer room, where the transport team was based. A man Anne didn't recognize sat at a round table by a bank of lockers, looking at his phone. He was in his forties, she guessed, and wearing standard-issue scrubs. An open can of energy drink sat in front of him. "I'm looking for Luke Merritt."

"I think he's over in the ER." The man scratched his forearm, where he had a tattoo of an arrow. "You can check for him there."

"Thanks. I'll try it."

Anne turned and walked downstairs and toward the ER, which was in the back of the hospital over by Records. As usual, the emergency room was a hive of activity, with doctors and nurses scurrying around. Anne made a loop around the hallways and decided the ambulance bay was her best bet, so she went out toward the big doors and found Luke Merritt smoking a cigarette under the overhang by the ambulance ramp. He was looking at his phone, and he looked up at Anne and then back down.

"Luke?" Now that she was here, Anne wasn't sure exactly what she was hoping to say to him. He wasn't a tall man, but he had tightly bunched muscles and a shaved head.

"Yeah?" He looked up at her again and blinked his eyes several times in rapid succession. That was one of his tics, and part of the reason many people found him strange, though it wasn't something he could control.

"I'm Anne Mabry. We met at the discharge area a few weeks ago."

He nodded but didn't say anything, blinking again. He held his phone in one hand and his cigarette in the other.

"I know you were working in the Labor and Delivery ward yesterday," she started.

"I work all over the hospital," Luke said. "Wherever they need me."

"That's true," Anne said. "I'm kind of like that myself. I go wherever they tell me to go. But I saw you on the L&D floor yesterday. Well, I'm sure you heard about that terrible theft that happened there—someone stole medication right out of the Pyxis machine." Anne watched him as she said this, hoping to see if he reacted in any way, but he just continued looking at her, unmoved. "I was wondering if you might have seen anything, since you were there about the right time," Anne said.

"Anything like what?" His voice was deep, raspy. "Like someone carrying a crowbar toward the machine?"

He blinked several times again. Was that meant to be a joke? Did he really think a crowbar had been used? Or was he trying to throw her off?

Anne tried to keep her voice level. "Anyone acting suspiciously. Or, I don't know, anything that seemed strange to you."

"I already spoke with the police." Luke grunted a bit, which would have seemed strange except that she recognized it as another one of his involuntary tics. It had happened a lot in their previous conversation.

"I know the police are looking into it," Anne said. Garrison had asked her to be discreet, so she couldn't come out and say that she was investigating too. "It's just that, because I was the one who found the machine broken into, I feel kind of responsible. So I'm just trying to see what I can find out. I know you were there, so I was wondering if you might have seen anything odd."

Instead of answering, Luke grunted again, and then he tossed his cigarette on to the ground and stubbed it out with his toe.

"I've got to get back to work." He turned and walked inside. Somewhere off in the distance, Anne heard a siren, and she figured she should move out of the way before the ambulance arrived. She headed inside too. Luke had already vanished, disappearing somehow into the busy emergency room. Anne puzzled over his reaction as she walked through the frenetic hallways, weaving around a young man slowly making his way down the hall uncertainly on crutches. She turned right, heading toward the lobby, and saw Dr. Chad Barnhardt coming out of one of the patient exam rooms.

"Hello, Anne."

"Hi, Dr. Barnhardt." Anne had spoken with him many times in the past and had always found him pleasant and witty, and he had a sterling reputation as a doctor.

"I heard you stumbled your way into another mystery yesterday," he said, closing the door softly behind him. "You seem to have a way of doing that."

"I just happened to be at the right place at the right time," Anne said. "Or maybe the wrong place, depending on how to you look at it."

"It's terrible, isn't it? It's just..."

He seemed to be struggling for words. Anne wasn't sure she'd ever seen the confident doctor at a loss.

"I keep finding myself asking who would do such a thing," Anne said.

"Someone truly desperate," he said. "You'd have to be deep in the throes of addiction to risk breaking into the machine like that. And it's happening more and more."

"Addiction, you mean?"

He nodded. "Reliance on opioids. Overdose deaths have gone up sharply in the past year or so. We've seen more and more patients brought in for overdose in recent months, and so many of them are too far gone for us to be able to do much to help."

"That must be terrible," she said.

"It's tragic." Dr. Barnhardt didn't mince words. "And what makes me crazy is that it's entirely preventable too. There's no reason we should be prescribing so many of these drugs in the first place."

"You don't think they should be prescribed at all?"

"Well, no, of course there are times when painkillers are necessary. When a patient is just out of surgery, for instance, or in serious pain after an injury or illness. But we need to be more careful, if you ask me, or we end up where we are now—with a national opioid crisis."

Anne hadn't heard anyone at the hospital use that phrase to describe the situation, but she supposed it probably fit.

"We've already administered several hundred doses of Narcan this year, just in the emergency room," he continued. "If that isn't the sign of a crisis, I don't know what is."

Anne was familiar with the drug. It was a powerful antidote that could often help stop accidental overdose. It came in a simple nasal spray and was designed so that anyone—from first responders to friends and family to bystanders—could administer it quickly and easily to anyone showing signs of overdose. Anne had looked into it a few years back when Nick had been staying with them "just until he got on his feet." If administered early enough in an overdose, it could save lives.

"I know a lot of people carry Narcan around, just in case," Anne said. Shirley carried it, as did many of the doctors and nurses and EMTs around the hospital.

"Absolutely. I do, even when I'm not on duty. Most of the staff here does too. You never know when you're going to encounter someone who will need it. And it can be life-saving. But it's not the same thing as never getting patients hooked on the drugs in the first place." He gave her a crooked smile. "But I suppose that would take one of your miracles."

Dr. Barnhardt, a by-the-book medical professional, was skeptical of claims of miracles, but Anne had seen them firsthand, more times than she could count. Tumors mysteriously vanished. Patients mysteriously healed. Children brought back from the brink.

"In that case, it's a good thing that miracles do happen," Anne said.

Dr. Barnhardt gave her a sad smile. She wasn't sure if that was better or worse than telling her outright that he disagreed.

"In any case, I'm hopeful they'll find out who broke into that machine," Dr. Barnhardt said. Down the hall, a nurse called to him, and he nodded and turned back to Anne. "Gotta run."

"We'll find the person," Anne said, watching him rush down the hallway. She looked down at her watch and saw that it was now a few minutes past twelve, so she hurried through the emergency room and back out into the lobby. Peggy looked up gratefully as she approached the front desk.

"Sorry I'm a few minutes late," Anne said.

"Don't worry about it." Peggy flashed a genuine smile. "I had a big breakfast, so I'm not even all that hungry. But I'll go see what the cafeteria has today." She pushed herself up and grabbed her ID, which was sitting on the desk, and slung it around her neck. "It's been pretty quiet. Which probably means it's about to get nuts in here. Sorry in advance."

Anne laughed and sat down at the desk, and Peggy went off, whistling as she walked away. Just then a man approached, asking for information about his mother, who was recovering from hip replacement surgery. Anne directed him to the orthopedics wing and then handled a few phone calls before she was able to think about what her next step should be. She wanted to watch the security camera footage as soon as she could. She got off at two. Lili had her class tonight, so Anne had to pick Addie up from gymnastics camp at four thirty, but she had some time before then.

She pulled out her phone and sent a group text to Evelyn, Shirley, and Joy: I HAVE THE SECURITY CAMERA FOOTAGE. WHO WANTS TO WATCH IT WITH ME WHEN I GET OFF MY SHIFT?

The replies came quick: I'M IN, from Joy. I'LL MAKE IT IF I CAN, from Shirley. COME WATCH IT HERE, from Evelyn.

MIRACLES & MYSTERIES of MERCY HOSPITAL

That was perfect. Few people went into the records room, so they could watch it there and still be discreet, as Garrison had requested.

SEE YOU IN RECORDS AT 2, Anne wrote back.

Anne answered phones and directed visitors to the right rooms until Peggy came back, a dewy cup of iced coffee in her hand.

"How was it?"

"Not too busy. Just the usual."

"Thank you for covering me." Peggy set the coffee down on the desk and slid into the chair when Anne stood up.

"Anytime. Happy to help." Anne spent the rest of her shift helping with discharge duty. As anxious as she was to start reviewing the security camera footage, her mind kept going back to the conversations she'd had that day with Olga and with Luke. Olga had lied to her, she was pretty sure, but the security camera footage would make it clear one way or the other. Luke hadn't lied to her, but he had refused to answer her questions. Was that because he had something to hide? Or just because she wasn't an official and he wasn't obligated to? But why wouldn't he answer her, if he was innocent? Why wouldn't he want to clear his name, if he had nothing to hide?

Anne didn't want to jump to conclusions. She didn't want to fall victim to the same trap Mandy and Polly had. Sure, Luke wasn't the most charming guy in the world, and he had some behaviors that put people off, but they weren't his fault, and they didn't mean he was guilty.

But it was an odd career change, wasn't it? To go from being a bouncer at a seedy club to a transport at a hospital? How often did people make that kind of a career move? From one place where drugs flowed freely to…well, to another? It didn't seem like it could be a total coincidence. Could it?

Anne couldn't shake the sense that something wasn't right. Was there any truth to what Mandy and Polly had insinuated earlier? Was it possible that Luke had taken the job at the hospital to get easier access to medications, which he would then sell to the club? It was possible. It was pure speculation, but it was possible.

Anne needed to find out more. She thought through her options as she pushed a young mother and her newborn baby toward the discharge exit. Anne chatted with the new mother about how beautiful her baby was and how hard the first weeks could be but how worth it they were, but the whole time, her mind was working its way around an idea, examining it from every angle, trying to decide whether it was a good idea or not. No, it was probably terrible. It made no sense.

But then again, talking to Luke hadn't yielded any result. She needed to find out whether there was any possibility Mandy and Polly were right. And she couldn't think of a better way to do it than this.

After her shift, she scooped up her things, tucked the binder under her arm and the thumb drive into her purse, and then made her way down to Records. Joy and Shirley were already gathered around Evelyn's desk, chatting.

Stacia was typing away at her computer, wearing giant noise-canceling headphones.

"Is this okay?" Anne glanced at Stacia. She didn't want her to overhear.

"She doesn't hear anything with those headphones on," Evelyn said. Everything on Evelyn's desk was arranged perfectly—the lamp and keyboard and monitor angled just right, the paper in precise stacks, even the pens in the jar organized neatly. "I think it's fine. I told her you all would be coming here to help me with something."

"Let's see this footage," said Shirley, gesturing for Anne to insert the thumb drive into Evelyn's computer. Anne pulled the drive out and plugged it in, and when she opened the file, a black-and-white image appeared on the screen. It showed the hallway outside the C-section recovery room.

"That must be the camera just down from the nurses' station," Shirley observed, and Anne nodded. The station was out of the field of view, but you could see the doors to several of the patient rooms, as well as the recovery room on the left. The hallway kept going toward the top of the frame. Hayley, a young nurse, was frozen on the screen, walking toward the nurses' station. The time stamp in the lower right corner said 11:20. Ten minutes or so before the beginning of the time frame they suspected, then.

"Where is the surgical supply closet?" Anne asked.

"Around the corner," Shirley said, pointing to the top left of the screen. "Just outside the operating rooms. Why?"

"Garrison told me they found a ribbon retractor in the trash can next to the machine. It was from a C-section kit that went missing earlier in the day."

"Really?" Shirley asked.

"Garrison seemed to think that it wouldn't be that hard to get into the supply closet," Anne said.

"He's right," Shirley confirmed. "There's a code on the door, but pretty much everyone knows it."

"But that means the thief is someone who knows a bit about the medical tools and where to find them," Joy said.

"Yes, but, as Garrison pointed out, that's pretty much everyone," Anne said. "Anyone who's spent any amount of time on the floor and was paying attention could have noticed the tools and where they come from. Luke has no doubt transported used bins of surgical equipment to the sanitizing room, and Olga has been inside all the rooms where the tools are used."

"Luke?" Shirley cocked her head. "Is he a suspect?"

Anne realized she had mentioned him to Joy but hadn't updated the others. She quickly explained that she'd seen him near the recovery room just before the theft was discovered.

"I suppose they're looking for fingerprints on the ribbon retractor?" Joy asked.

"Garrison said the police were doing that. My guess is that anyone who had access to a C-section kit also had access to rubber gloves, but we'll see," Anne said.

"Let's play the video. Maybe that will tell us something." Joy said.

Anne pushed play, and Hayley began moving back toward the nurses' station. Several people—visitors, most likely—walked down the hall.

"Let's speed it up," Joy suggested. Anne nodded. It would take forever to watch this thing in real time. Now each person moved at double speed. She'd never realized how busy this hallway was—was every hallway in the hospital this heavily trafficked? There went Shirley, checking in on the patients.

"That's Paige, heading into the recovery room," Shirley said, pointing to a nurse on the screen. "That must be when we were about to move the patient out of there." A moment later, Shirley appeared again, and she also went into the room.

"The machine was definitely closed at this point, because I used it when I went in there," Shirley said. "Dr. Perez had prescribed Demerol for this patient, and I gave it to her just before we moved her."

More people moved about and then, a few minutes later, Shirley and Paige emerged, Shirley pushing the rolling bed, Paige gripping the IV. The woman on the bed looked completely drained and overwhelmed. They led her off the bottom of the screen.

"So we know that the theft happened sometime between now"— Evelyn pointed at the time stamp again, which read 11:33:23—"and when Anne discovered the machine open, around twelve thirty."

"Which means that we just need to see who goes into the room in that time," Joy said, nodding.

So much activity—nurses chatting and laughing, patients being wheeled to their postpartum rooms, cradling newborns, anxious-looking visitors, doctors. The kind of stuff you would expect to see in a busy hospital corridor. Then, at 11:48, someone turned in to the hallway and went into the recovery room.

"Back up. Who was that?" Joy asked.

Anne reversed and paused the footage. You could only see the back of the person, but it was a woman dressed in scrubs.

"That looks like Miranda," Shirley said. "But I can't say for sure from the back."

"Who's Miranda?" Joy asked.

"Miranda Martel," Anne said. She'd met her a few times, and she seemed nice.

"She's a nurse who works on the floor," Evelyn said. "Keep going."

Anne played the footage again, and Miranda was in the room for three minutes before she emerged once more and strolled into the hallway, continuing toward the top of the screen. Anne paused it.

"That's enough time to get medication out of the machine," Shirley said. "Or to break in."

"Why would she be using the Pyxis machine in the recovery room, though?" Anne asked. "If there were no patients there?"

"Maybe the one at the other end of the hallway was busy. Maybe she was closer to this end." Shirley shrugged.

"Or maybe she didn't want to be seen," Joy added. "She would have known that room is often empty."

"It's hard to say." Shirley's brow wrinkled. "But if she actually used that machine, that would be recorded in the Pyxis records."

"I'll check into that," Anne said. "But even if she did legitimately use the machine, that doesn't mean she didn't also break in, does it?"

"I suppose not," Shirley said.

"So she's on the list of suspects," Joy said. "Let's see who else goes in."

Anne pressed play again and saw several people she recognized walking through the hallway. There went Shirley again, checking on patients. Anne recognized Dr. Perez, an OB/GYN who delivered a lot of babies at Mercy. She wore high heels and a pencil skirt under her lab coat and stared down at her phone as she walked. Anne could never understand how she managed to spend so much time in stilettos, but more power to her. There went Maxine, another nurse Anne had met, and a guy from maintenance. Anne didn't know his name, but she'd seen him before.

No one went into the recovery room again until 11:55, when Olga Dotov walked down the hallway from the top of the screen and pushed her cart into the recovery room. She pulled the door closed behind her, but it swung open again.

"So she was definitely there," Joy said. "Even though she said she wasn't."

"And she closed the door, or tried to," Shirley said. "So for some reason she didn't want to be seen."

"But wait. I saw her coming out of the room when I walked past at twelve thirty," Anne said. "Was she in there that whole time?"

"Let's see," Evelyn said. Olga didn't emerge for nearly eight minutes.

"What could she have been doing in there for so long?" Anne asked.

"Probably cleaning up the space where the last patient had been," Shirley said. "Emptying the trash, sanitizing the whole area. That's what she normally does in that room."

"On the other hand, it's enough time to break into the machine," Evelyn said. "And clean it out."

Anne nodded and let the video run. A few minutes after Olga, a man in a white coat walked down the hallway from the top of the screen and ducked into the room.

"Who's that?" Evelyn asked.

"Some doctor," Anne said. "But I couldn't tell who."

"Dark hair, male, medium height. That's about all you can tell from the back," Shirley said. "Could be anyone. Let's see if we can tell more about him when he comes back out."

The doctor was in the room less than a minute and a half when he emerged again and started walking back the way he came. Anne froze the video and studied him.

"That's Dr. Lyle," Shirley said. "An anesthesiologist. He did two epidurals for my patients yesterday."

"Brendan Lyle?" Anne knew him. His parents had been members of St. Michael's for decades. Anne had been his Sunday school teacher when he was a teenager. His father was on the board of elders. Brendan had been married at the church, and Ralph had done the ceremony, followed by a reception at a luxury hotel nearby. Brendan hadn't been involved in the church personally in many years beyond the obligatory Christmas and Easter services, but the few instances Anne had spoken with him, he was kind and thoughtful and charming. She'd run into him occasionally at the hospital, and he'd smiled and asked about her family every time.

"What would an anesthesiologist be doing in the recovery room?" Joy asked.

"He wouldn't be giving epidurals, for sure. But he could have been investigating to see if the patient he'd anesthetized was there to check on." Shirley shrugged. "I suppose it could have been anything.

Maybe he needed a quiet place for a phone call. We all duck into unused rooms sometimes for that kind of thing."

"It doesn't seem like a minute and a half would be enough time to pry that machine open and grab the medication," Anne said.

"No, it sure doesn't," Evelyn said. "And besides, why would an anesthesiologist need to break into a Pyxis? They're the ones in charge of anesthesia. They control the most powerful drugs."

"Are the medications used in an epidural kept in the Pyxis?" Anne asked.

Shirley nodded. "But the anesthesiologists all have access to the machines. So if he needed an epidural, he could just punch it in and get it."

Anne thought this all through. He seemed the least likely suspect so far. But still, he had been in the room, there was no denying that.

"I'll see if I can find out more about him," Anne said. "In the meantime, let's keep going."

On the screen, people passed within the frame.

"There you are again, Shirley." Evelyn pointed at the little figure of Shirley. "You're the busiest person on this floor."

Shirley gave a rueful smile.

At 12:24, Luke Merritt appeared on the bottom of the screen, pushing the empty wheelchairs Anne had seen him with. But then, instead of walking past the room, he ducked in. He also pulled the door closed behind him, but it snapped right back open.

"Why is he going in there?" Anne wondered aloud.

"Maybe he was asked to move a bed?" But by the tone of Shirley's voice, she didn't believe it herself. Three minutes later, he came out of the room, no bed in sight. He stepped into the hallway, looked around, and then walked over toward the wheelchairs and started pushing them back the way he'd come.

"That's shady," Evelyn said.

"There might be a good reason he went in there," Joy said, but she didn't really sound like she believed it.

It sure looked bad. It wasn't proof he was guilty, but it certainly didn't look good.

"Look, here comes Olga again," Shirley said, as the housekeeper ducked back into the room. She didn't have her cart this time; she didn't have anything in her hands, actually.

"What is she doing going back in there?"

This time, Olga was only in the room for a few seconds—less than a minute, according to the time stamp at the bottom. But whatever she was doing inside, she walked out just as Anne appeared, carrying the flowers down the hall.

"There you are," Evelyn said, pointing at the image of Anne. She traced her finger along the screen, following Anne as she walked to the top of the screen.

"I took them to room 321. I chatted with the family for a few minutes," Anne said. "And then came back out and down the hallway."

"Which means we should be seeing you come back right about…" Joy let her voice trail off.

"There you are." Shirley pointed as Anne returned. She walked down the hallway, and then, in the video, it was clear that something caught her eye to the right, and she stopped suddenly.

"Good reflexes," Joy said, smiling. "How did you manage to stop so quickly?"

On screen, Anne backed up. The camera angle made it hard to read facial expressions, but it was clear something had surprised her, shocked her enough to stop her in her tracks. Then she turned and walked into the recovery room, and, only twenty seconds later, she came back out and rushed toward the nurses' station, off-screen.

"Anyone who sees that has to know that you aren't under suspicion," Evelyn said. "There was no way you were faking that surprise."

"And we know who our suspects are," Shirley said. "We have Miranda the nurse, Luke the transport, Dr. Lyle the anesthesiologist, and Olga the housekeeper. Those are the only four people who went into the room. So it has to be one of them."

"Plus Anne," Evelyn added. "Technically, she went into the room, though we know you didn't do it, Anne. We just need to find out who did so we can prove that."

"I think it was Luke," Joy said. "He had no reason to go into that room, and didn't he look guilty when he came out?"

"But what about Olga?" Evelyn asked. "She lied to Anne and said she wasn't there, when it's clear in the footage that she was."

Shirley didn't venture a guess, but Anne could see on her face that she had an opinion of her own.

Anne nodded, but she was thinking about something else. "Olga was the last one in there," she said slowly.

"Right," Evelyn agreed. "Her second time around."

"If it was one of the people who went in earlier—or even if it was Olga the first time—then at least one other person went into that room *after* the machine was broken into," Anne said. "Did they just not see that the machine was opened?"

"Or did they see it and not report it?" Shirley was nodding.

"Or did they see it open and help themselves?" Joy added.

"That would explain why they're not anxious to talk to Anne," Shirley said.

"But there could also be other reasons they're not anxious to talk to Anne," Joy said. "Or the police."

"Well, at least we now know for sure who our suspects are," Anne said. "We'll just have to find out more about each of them."

"At least one of them knows more than they're saying," Joy added.

There was a beat of silence before Shirley said, "I'm afraid I have to get back."

"I should probably get back to work as well," Joy said.

Anne took the thumb drive back and slipped it into her pocket, and then she thanked her friends as she walked with Shirley and Joy out into the lobby. Shirley hurried off to her shift, but Anne walked with Joy toward the gift shop. She was thinking through what she'd seen, and what had happened that day, and the idea she'd had earlier was taking shape in her mind. It might be a bad idea, she realized. In fact, it probably was. But still. If there was any chance...

"Do you want to run an errand with me when you're done with your shift?" Anne had the words out before she could change her mind.

"The depends." They stood in front of the gift shop, and Joy stepped aside so that a couple holding hands could enter. Lacy was on duty, so they didn't need to rush back inside. "What kind of errand?"

"I want to go to the nightclub where Luke Merritt used to work."

"Oh, I don't think the clubs are much fun midafternoon," Joy deadpanned. "I think you'll need to wait until tonight if you're going to have any fun at all."

Anne laughed. "Not to dance. I want to talk to the people he used to work for. With. See what they have to say about him."

"Do you think anyone will be there in the middle of the day?"

"I honestly don't know," Anne said. "Believe it or not, I don't spend a lot of time at nightclubs."

"I'm shocked. That seems like it would totally be your scene."

"I guess you learn something new every day." Anne smiled. "So do you want to come?"

"I'm certainly not about to let you go there alone," Joy said. "If you're headed there, I'm coming too. Someone has to keep you out of trouble."

Anne chuckled. "So I'll see you in about twenty minutes?"

"I'll meet you by the parking garage."

Chapter Five

ANNE MET HER FRIEND a while later, and they drove Anne's car over to the east side of town and parked on a small strip of cracked cement behind the black brick building. The structures on either side were run-down warehouses, and several auto body shops were sprinkled between clubs and bars.

A wave of humidity hit Anne as soon as she stepped out of her car. Did they have to paint the building black? Didn't that attract the sun? Joy walked toward Anne, her slim slacks and low pumps incongruous in this run-down parking lot, and together they walked around to what Anne assumed was the front of the building, though it was hard to tell, toward a metal door that faced the street. Graffiti graced several of the buildings on the block. A neon sign spelled out SHADE, though the light was off in the afternoon sun.

"Do we just go in?" Joy asked, gesturing toward the door.

"Let's see if it's unlocked." Anne reached out and pulled on the handle, and she wasn't surprised to find it locked. The club was clearly not open yet. There was a buzzer mounted on the wall by the door, and Anne pressed the button. Joy smiled up at a security camera overhead. A moment later, the door buzzed, and Anne pulled it open and stepped inside.

"At least it's cool in here," Joy said, as they stepped into a dark corridor. The walls were painted black too, and the pendant lights did not illuminate much through their black shades. To the right, a large room opened up with a bar along one wall. To the left was a series of doors. There was no one to meet them, though someone obviously knew they were here.

Anne walked down the hallway cautiously, Joy just a step beside her. She passed bathrooms and a coat check before she got to a room marked OFFICE. She knocked gently on the door and heard a noise that sounded like a cross between a grunt and a cough.

"What was that?" Joy asked.

Anne wasn't sure, but she reached for the handle and pushed the door open anyway. After the dark hallway, the fluorescent lights in this room were far too bright. Anne blinked against them and stepped inside to find two men seated behind metal desks. Computers and piles of papers sat on the desks, and one wall of the room was lined with filing cabinets.

"Yeah?" The older man, sitting closer to the door, chewed gum and was looking at them. He had brushed his dyed, too-brown hair across the top of his head in a futile attempt to cover his bald spot.

"Hi there. I'm Anne Mabry, and this is my friend Joy Atkins." Both men continued to stare at her, so she pressed on. "We're working with Mercy Hospital on an inquiry"—it was technically true, and she hoped sounded somewhat official—"and we were hoping to learn more about a man who used to work here. Luke Merritt."

"Oh yeah, Luke. Good guy." The younger man spoke this time from his desk at the rear of the small room. He had slicked-back dark hair, and his paunch strained the fabric of his button-down.

"Can you tell me anything about Luke's employment here at Shade?" Anne asked.

The older one shrugged. "He came to work. Did his job. Never gave us any problems. What more do you need to know?"

"What was his job, exactly?" Joy asked.

"Bouncer," the younger one said. "Guarded the door, checked ID, kept the riffraff out."

"And you said he was good at his job?" Anne asked.

"He's a big guy." The older one shrugged. "He was good at keeping rowdy patrons in line."

"Would you say you have a lot of rowdy patrons?" Joy asked.

"It's a nightclub." He picked up a pen and began twirling it in his fingers. "As the night goes on, sometimes people have a bit too much to drink, things get out of hand. Par for the course. Nothing every other club in this city doesn't deal with."

It sounded horrible to Anne. Did people really come here for fun?

"And you said Luke was good at defusing situations?" Joy asked.

"Defuse." The younger one snorted. "That's one way to put it."

"He was good at throwing them out." The older man leaned back in his desk chair, twisting it a bit from side to side. "He could grab a guy by the collar before they even knew what was happening."

"Did you ever have any problems with Luke?" Anne asked. "Anything in his work record that raised red flags?"

"Not really."

"What were the circumstances of his departure?" Joy asked.

"You mean, why'd he quit?" The younger one asked. Anne nodded. "Said he wanted better hours, more stable career path, that kind of thing. Couldn't argue with him there. Throwing drunks out on the street isn't the kind of thing you want to do your whole life. Was sorry to see him go, though."

"Does Luke still have contact with anyone at the club?" Anne asked.

"Sometimes." The older one narrowed his eyes. "Why? Is he in trouble?"

"Not necessarily," Anne said quickly. She wasn't sure how much to say. "It's just that we're investigating an incident at the hospital and wanted some more background."

"What kind of incident?" the younger one asked.

Instead of answering, Anne asked, "Are you aware of any substances that pass through the club that are, well, less-than-legal?"

"I think we've answered enough questions." The older one straightened and started to push himself up to standing.

"We'd better get going—" Joy started to say, but Anne cut her off.

"Do you know if Luke was ever involved in making, well, deals?" Anne had to try one more time.

"It's time for you to go." Both men were now standing, and she saw that the younger one was much taller than she'd guessed.

"Thank you for your help," Anne said, and she quickly turned and walked out of the office, just a step behind Joy. They both hurried down the dark hallway again and back out onto the sidewalk. Neither of them stopped moving until they were in Anne's car and driving back toward the hospital.

"They sure didn't like the suggestion that drugs were used in the club, did they?" Anne said. Her heartbeat was only just now starting to return to normal.

"No, but you can see why," Joy said. "Even if it's true, it's illegal—they couldn't exactly admit to it, now could they?"

"I didn't get the sense those two admit to much of anything, true or not," Anne said. "Why would anyone want to hang out at a place like that?"

"Different strokes," Joy said. "I suppose there are a lot of people who would struggle to understand why I spend so much time in my garden."

Anne was one of those people. She had no success with plants, personally, but Joy loved her garden and coaxed the most amazing blooms out of her small patch of earth. It wasn't fair of Anne to judge people who enjoyed spending time at clubs…but it wasn't her cup of tea, that was for sure.

"On the plus side, we learned a few things," Joy said. "Big, strong Luke is used to roughing people up."

"Which would mean he probably wouldn't have too much trouble jimmying that machine open," Anne said. "They said he left the club for better hours and a more stable job, which may or may not be the whole story."

"Right," Joy said. "I'm sure working in the hospital is more stable than being a bouncer. But is that the whole reason? Could he have another, ulterior motive for wanting to work so closely with the medical establishment?"

"We don't know, but we do know that the club owners reacted strongly to the idea that there might be drugs flowing through the club."

"They reacted strongly, but they didn't deny it," Joy said. "Which they probably would have done if they knew it wasn't true."

"And they also told us that they still have contact with Luke from time to time. It doesn't seem like the kind of place former employees just drop in to hang out," Anne said. "If he's dropping by to check in, there's probably a reason. A strong financial one, I would guess."

"Overall, I'd say Luke Merritt should stay right at the top of our suspect list," Joy said.

Anne couldn't agree more.

After Anne dropped Joy off at the hospital, Anne was on her way back to North Charleston. Twenty minutes later, she pulled up in front of the gym, a former warehouse building that had been ret-rofitted with modern gymnastics equipment. Anne always found the space overwhelming, with kids spinning around on parallel bars and turning cartwheels on the springy floor. Anne walked in and found Addie bouncing on the trampoline with several other girls, and it took some time to coax her down, but as she climbed into the car, she told Anne about how they'd worked on back handsprings today. As they drove, Addie moved on from chattering about gym-nastics to talking about a cruise her friend Cora had just come back from.

"She brought us all shells." Addie pulled a small scallop shell from her pocket. "She says she found them on the beach in Mexico."

"That was nice of her." Anne drove through the familiar streets near the house, glad to have Addie back in the car once again. As much as she loved having Lili home, she missed the day-to-day interaction with Addie. "You remembered to say thank you?"

"Yes, Nana." Addie rolled her eyes. "Can we go to Mexico sometime?"

Anne laughed. "I very much hope we can make that happen at some point." They didn't have the budget for that this year, that was for sure. But it might be interesting to have Addie's ideas about the trip, in case they didn't go with Ralph's idea of a house in the mountains. "I'm actually working on planning our summer vacation right now. We can't go to Mexico, sadly, but if you have ideas, I'd love to hear them."

"Disney World!"

Anne started as Addie shouted. "Wow. You didn't have to think about that one, did you?"

"I've wanted to go there my whole life. My friend Cecily went over spring break, and she stayed in a Lion King room and got to meet Merida and swim in the most amazing pool ever with a slide. She even got to ride Space Mountain, which she said isn't even a mountain but a roller coaster inside a ball."

"She got to meet who?" Hearing the excitement in Addie's voice, Anne realized she'd made a mistake. They couldn't afford a trip to Disney World, at least not the kind of vacation Addie was thinking of. She'd looked into it a few years back, and she'd been shocked at how much it all cost. You could buy a small car for the same price. The park tickets alone would use up their whole budget, never mind the hotels and food and inevitable souvenirs. Was that the kind of vacation parents were expected to give kids these days? When Lili was young, they'd thought it was a treat to go camping for a long weekend.

"Merida. From *Brave*. And Raya from *Raya and the Last Dragon*. Belle has a restaurant where the dishes sing to you, and Cecily got to go there too. And there's a Frozen ride at Epcot that she said is *amazing*."

"That does sound pretty great." Anne tried to figure out how to say this gently. "And I really hope we can take you there someday. But I don't know that we can do that this summer."

"How about spring break?"

Hearing the naked hope in Addie's voice, Anne's heart broke just a little.

"I don't know that it's going to happen for spring break either," Anne said. "Disney World is quite expensive."

"I can save up my allowance. How many weeks' allowance would it take?"

Anne wanted to cry. "Quite a few, I'm afraid."

"Okay. Maybe I could get a job so I could help pay for it?"

"I love that you want to help," Anne said. "Thank you for that. Disney World may be something we all need to save up for, and I'm glad to know you want to go. But we may need to find something a bit less expensive for this summer."

"Okay." And just like that, Addie was singing a song Anne recognized from one of the *Descendants* films, and seemed to have moved on. Anne was grateful for her good attitude. Though she knew kids survived disappointment every day, it was still hard to say no to something your grandchild wanted. And maybe someday she would be able to take Addie. But this year was not that year, unfortunately. She drove home, trying to come up with something better, and by the time she pulled into the driveway, she was itching to do some research into mountain cabins, but she had to get started on dinner.

Lili arrived just as Anne was setting the grilled swordfish on the table.

"Hi, Mom. That smells delicious." Lili was still wearing her fatigues, and her hair was pulled back into a tight regulation ponytail.

"Why don't you stay and eat? There's plenty." Anne had also made green beans and roasted baby potatoes, Lili's favorite, hoping she could convince her to stick around.

"I wish we could, but I have to study tonight. I have a test later this week."

"You have to eat. This will be faster and easier than making something at home."

Lili gave her an apologetic smile. "I promised Addie I'd take her through the McDonald's drive-through. She's really into the toys they're giving out in the Happy Meals right now."

So much of what Lili had just said upset Anne, but she bit her tongue. Lili was Addie's mom. If she wanted to feed her fast food instead of good, healthy, home-cooked food, it wasn't her place to say anything.

"Can I give you some for you to eat?"

"Sure." Lili let out a breath. "That would be great. Thanks, Mom."

Anne went down the hallway to Addie's room—technically the guest room now that Addie lived with her mom again, but to Anne it would always be Addie's room—to let Addie know it was time to go home, and then into the kitchen to get a Tupperware container. She brought it back out to the table and filled it with fish, green beans, and potatoes.

"Thanks again." Lili took the container. "I really appreciate this, and your picking Addie up today."

"It's never a bother," Anne said. Addie's father wasn't in the picture, and it was a lot for Lili to juggle on her own. Anne was glad to be able to be so involved in her granddaughter's life.

"Guess what, Mom?" Addie sat on the ground as she slipped her shoes on. "We're going on vacation, but Nana says we can't go to Disney World this summer and probably not spring break either."

"I know we're going on vacation," Lili said. "In just a few weeks." Lili turned back to Anne. "Have you figured out where yet?"

"I've been looking at beach houses, but I'm not really finding a lot at this point. Your dad wants to go to the mountains, so I'm going to focus on that now."

"That sounds nice."

"You'd be okay with a cabin in the mountains?"

"Sure." Anne heard the hesitation in her voice.

"But…"

"It's not that I don't want to go there," Lili said. "It's just that that's more Dad's thing than mine."

Oh. Anne didn't want to plan a trip somewhere Lili didn't want to go. "In that case, what sounds good to you?"

She cocked her head and then said, "One of my friends in my platoon just got back from a week in California. They saw San Francisco and Yosemite and the redwoods and then went south to the beaches and did the whole Hollywood thing. She said it was pretty great. That may be over the budget, but it sounded fun to me."

Anne hadn't been to California in decades, and she had only been in the southern part of the state for an old friend's wedding. She'd never toured Yosemite or seen the redwoods. They were supposed to be amazing. And she'd never visited San Francisco. The city was supposed to be like a jewel box perched on a hill.

"That's an interesting idea." Anne thought that might be over their budget—the flights alone would be challenging—but she didn't want to tell Lili so until she'd looked into it. If that was what Lili wanted to do, she could at least see if it was possible. "I'll do some research."

"It would be really fun, and such a good experience for Addie."

Addie could learn about the gold rush and the 1906 earthquake and so much more. Anything that would be educational for Addie was always a win. It would be fun, and the kind of trip where they would make memories. They hadn't had a family vacation—all of them together—in years. Addie was growing up so fast, and who knew when Lili would be deployed next, or for how long. This could be the last summer vacation in a good while that they could all be together. Anne wanted it to be not just a week away but a wonderful time of making memories they would all cherish. Anne was going to make the most of this opportunity, no matter what.

"I'll do some more research tonight," Anne promised.

"Sounds good. Thanks again for picking her up, Mom."

"I'm happy to." Lili always sounded so apologetic when she picked Addie up, as if watching her was something that put Anne out. Anne didn't know how to make her understand that she considered it a joy, not a burden. "Anytime."

Lili helped Addie to her feet. "You ready, Adds?"

"Ready."

After they left, Anne and Ralph sat down to eat, and while the food was delicious, the meal was a little too quiet for her taste. When they were done, he cleaned up the kitchen while she sat down in front of her computer. She opened a web browser and searched for flights to California. Goodness. It was a long flight, but could it really cost that much? Maybe if they flew to Los Angeles instead of San Francisco? But that wasn't much better. But just look at those redwoods. Anne read blogs and travel websites that showed gloriously tall red-barked trees lining the coast. Incredible. And the photos of the Golden Gate Bridge, poking up through the fog—could that even be real? Was it actually that color? How did people live on those crazy hills?

California looked amazing. They could hike and swim and see waterfalls, and Addie would just love a visit to the Disney Studios tour.... It would be the trip of a lifetime, which was exactly what Anne longed for. Plus this was what Lili wanted. Wasn't it worth stretching a bit to make the most of this opportunity? Who knew when it would come around again?

But what about Ralph? She'd like to make Lili happy, but she also wanted to do what Ralph wanted. She pulled up a website that listed mountain cabins and started scrolling. But she quickly got frustrated. So many of the rentals were already booked. As she scrolled, she got more and more disheartened. She should stop this. She should step away for now. She sighed and closed her browser window. But as soon as she stopped looking into vacations, her mind drifted back to the mystery that had kept her busy for most of the day. After what she had seen in the security camera footage and what she had heard about Luke, she wanted to find out more. And if Luke wasn't willing to talk with her about what he knew, there had to be another way to learn more about him.

Anne opened up a new browser window. She typed in the name LUKE MERRITT and began to sort through the results. The name was common enough that she found several social media profiles, though none of them seemed to be the right one. She did, however, find an article in the *Charleston Times* from 2019 that mentioned him. DOZENS ARRESTED IN STING AT POPULAR NIGHTCLUB, the headline read. Oh boy. Anne clicked on the link and read that the police had entered the club after a months-long sting operation and uncovered evidence that many illegal drugs, including several popular opioids, cocaine, and quaaludes had been distributed on the premises. During the raid, police had arrested patrons in possession of illegal substances, as well as a number of staff, including the long-time bouncer Luke Merritt, who had pled guilty.

This was the man they had wandering around the hospital every day? Hadn't the HR department done any background checks on this guy?

Anne dug around some more, and she found out that Luke had served jail time. Here was solid evidence that the nightclub was a place where drugs were bought and sold, and Luke had a clear connection to it. What better way to make a little extra cash than to take the drugs from the hospital and sell them at the club? It would have been genius if it weren't so devious.

Still, she didn't have proof that Luke was her guy, and there were three other suspects. It could still be Olga, who had definitely lied to her about being in that recovery room. Or it could be Dr. Lyle or Miranda Martel, the nurse.

She googled the name Olga Dotov and found a Facebook page. It was mostly filled with photos of Olga and her son, who looked to be about ten. There they were at his fifth-grade graduation; in front of the church on Easter; at Christmas. There was no father in any of the pictures, and Anne wondered if he was…well, in the picture. There was nothing on the page that indicated she had been in recovery or had stolen drugs, but then, Anne supposed there wouldn't be.

Next, she googled Brendan Lyle. She found a bio for him on the hospital's website and read that he'd graduated from Yale. Anne remembered that his mother was so proud when he'd gotten in. She had slipped the word Yale into conversations the whole time Brendan was an undergraduate. It had been insufferable, actually. But Anne could understand the impulse. After he'd graduated, he'd gotten his MD at Johns Hopkins, according to the website, and then he'd done his residency in anesthesiology in Manhattan and his fellowship in Atlanta. Goodness, that was a lot of school. And no doubt a lot of money spent on all that education, though she supposed it paid off now. Anesthesiologists were among the highest paid doctors in medicine. Then again, they were responsible for dosing patients for surgery, which made their jobs one of the most dangerous. Still, as Anne clicked over to his Instagram page, it seemed like he was doing all right.

Dr. Lyle's social media looked like a commercial. There were shots of him and his beautiful blond wife on a beach and shots of them with two small sandy-haired boys. There were photos of his house, which Anne recognized as one of the iconic waterfront mansions right along Charleston Harbor, with its triple-decker balcony and its long side porch. It was painted a soft shade of pale green and had a direct view of the bay. There were pictures of him and his family on a boat, posing in front of a sporty new BMW, a photo of him crossing the finish line of a marathon—he looked like he was in so much pain; why would anyone willingly do that to himself?— pictures of him in a gym, bench-pressing an insane amount of weight, and pictures of him and his wife on a medieval bridge in some historic European town. Prague, according to the caption. Apparently Dr. Lyle didn't have to worry about whether he could scrape together enough pennies to buy domestic flights.

There was nothing about stealing drugs and no evidence of any kind of addiction. Again, though, that was hardly the kind of thing one would post about on social media. No mention of St. Michael's, though Anne wasn't surprised by that either. Anne did have a fleeting thought—was there any chance Dr. Lyle's lavish lifestyle was partially funded by selling the powerful opioids he had access to daily? But why would an anesthesiologist need to sell drugs to live like this? Anne did a quick google search and saw that the pay rate started at about $200,000 per year. That was the minimum. That would buy several vacations to Prague.

She moved on to Miranda Martel. A google search of her name brought up Miranda's Facebook page, and Anne scrolled through the posts and pictures. Miranda had shared photos of herself on a girl's weekend; holding a squirming puppy; on a date night with her husband, who Anne gathered was a firefighter. There was a shot of her sitting with a man in a wheelchair as he blew out candles on a birthday cake, nurses in scrubs around him, and of her teenage son wearing soccer cleats and shin guards and holding a shiny gold trophy. Anne didn't spot anything that gave her pause. Nothing that raised any red flags. But what was she expecting? What did she honestly think she would find?

"I'm about to turn in."

Anne jumped at the sound of Ralph's voice.

"Goodness. You scared me." She pivoted and saw that he had put on his pajamas. Where had the time gone?

"What are you working on so intently in here?" He stepped into the room and looked at her screen.

"I'm checking into the people who might have broken into that Pyxis machine."

"It's really bothering you, isn't it?"

"Of course it is," Anne said. "I just can't help thinking, whoever it is, they must have been really desperate to get those drugs, for whatever reason. And I just... I feel like if I figure out who it is, maybe I can help."

Ralph stepped closer, and then he stood behind her chair and draped his arms around her shoulders.

"You know it's not Nick, right?" he asked quietly. "Whoever took those drugs, it's not your brother."

"I know," Anne said. "But I can't help thinking..."

"Of course," Ralph said. He drew a deep breath and let it out slowly. And then, a moment later, he said, "Have you called him?"

She shook her head. "I just...he never answers my calls these days."

"That doesn't necessarily mean you shouldn't keep trying."

Anne nodded. Perhaps.

"Maybe try calling him tomorrow." Ralph leaned in and kissed her cheek. "For now, why don't you come to bed?"

Anne reluctantly closed her laptop and let Ralph lead her down the hallway. She'd see what else she could learn in the morning.

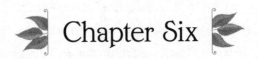

Chapter Six

ANNE SLEPT FITFULLY, AND SHE woke up before the sun Wednesday morning. Somewhere in the middle of the night when she'd been trying to fall back asleep, she'd realized what she needed to do next. Googling the four people who had gone into the recovery room hadn't provided her any insight, and talking to two of them hadn't yielded anything but more suspicion. She would still need to talk to Miranda and Dr. Lyle, but she also needed to look at the evidence that was already right in front of her. She had the binder that contained all the Pyxis records. Shirley and Evelyn both knew one of the nurses was suspected of stealing drugs from the machine. Was it Miranda? Anne guessed that looking at the Pyxis records would tell her one way or the other. If it was Miranda, then she became suspect number one. If not, then there was another person she needed to be on the lookout for.

But before she dove into the binder, Anne needed to start her day off by reading God's Word. No matter what was going on in her life, she found peace and serenity there. She was currently reading through the Old Testament, and she was now in 1 Samuel. Anne loved the dramatic history of God's chosen people, and she always marveled when reading about the ascent of King Saul to the throne. The people of Israel had demanded a king, and though Samuel had warned them against it, and even though it was contrary to God's plans for them, God allowed Saul to be anointed to rule over them. It was such a good reminder to Anne that God's will for His children was perfect, but He allowed people to make their own choices about whether they would seek His will and follow it. And He also allowed them to face the consequences of their mistakes, but He always helped them through them.

This morning, Anne's reading was from chapter sixteen, after King Saul had disobeyed God, even following a series of military victories. Because he disobeyed, Samuel had told Saul that God would appoint another king in his place, and God sent Samuel to find the one God had chosen. Samuel followed God's instructions, journeying to Bethlehem to find Jesse, and asking Jesse to line up his sons.

"When they arrived, Samuel saw Eliab and thought, 'Surely the LORD's anointed stands here before the LORD.' But the LORD said to Samuel, 'Do not consider his appearance or his height, for I have rejected him. The LORD does not look at the things people look at. People look at the outward appearance, but the LORD looks at the heart'" (1 Samuel 16:6–7).

People so often saw things that looked good on the outside—and generally could be perfectly fine—but if they were not what God had chosen, they weren't right. Eliab, son of Jesse, had looked how Samuel expected a king to look, but he wasn't the one God had chosen. Instead, Samuel asked Jesse to parade all his sons—each strong and faithful, each looking to Samuel like a potential king—but none of them were the one Samuel had been appointed to anoint. It wasn't until little David, the youngest, had been called in from the field—David, the son Jesse hadn't thought to even bring in to meet the prophet before this—that Samuel found the next king of Israel.

How often did people settle for what they thought God wanted for them instead of holding out for His best? How often did people see only the things that matched their own preconceptions, instead of asking to see things through God's eyes?

After she'd spent some time in prayer, asking God to help her see and judge with His eyes, looking at the things He cared about, Anne brewed a strong pot of coffee and sat down at the kitchen table with the binder and a notebook. She opened the binder's cover and looked down.

Goodness. Evelyn was right. The pages were just a series of tiny numbers and letters, one after another. How would she even begin to make sense of this?

She started by first noting that each entry had a user identification number at the top. That would be the nurse who accessed the system, she assumed. Anne would need to find a way to correlate the IDs with names of users, but she was sure there would be a way to do so.

Each entry also had the name beneath that, and Anne quickly realized they were the names of doctors who served in the labor and delivery unit. Emerson. Hassan. Alexander. Patel. Steadman. Perez. Chiu. They all worked on the unit regularly, and Anne had met many of them through the years. Those were the names of the doctors who prescribed each medication, then. There was a number in each entry for a diagnosis code—those would be easy to look up—as well as a space for a control number. It took some googling, but Anne eventually realized that this was the number assigned to each medication. This would tell her which drug had been prescribed. Each entry then also had a time and date that the machine had been accessed.

She flipped through the pages, one at a time, paying attention to the ID number of the person who had accessed the machine, which drug had been taken, how many pills had been removed, and the small number that indicated the amount left in the drawer after the medication was taken.

There were several dozen ID numbers that used the machine, but after scrutinizing the pages, Anne noticed some small discrepancies coming up with one user ID. It wasn't so much that you'd notice, unless you were looking for it. But the numbers were definitely off. After user 669277 used the machine, the pill counts were often a bit...well, different than they should be. On May 27, user 669277 had logged into the machine to retrieve a prescription of two oxycodone pills for a patient and had entered into the machine that there were fifteen pills left. But two hours later, when user 658256 had opened the same drawer to retrieve oxycodone for a different patient, she had taken two pills out and noted that there were only eleven pills left in the machine, and then, another hour later, a third user had taken one out and noted that there were only ten left. Somehow, two pills had gone missing between the first and second users. Had user 669277 taken them and lied about the number that was left? Recorded the number wrong? Or had everyone else somehow gotten it wrong?

The same thing had happened on May 29, when user 669277 had retrieved one hydrocodone for a patient and noted that there were thirty pills left in the drawer. But the next nurse to access the same drawer had noted that there were twenty-seven left after taking out one pill for her patient. Again, two pills had somehow gone missing.

Anne noticed this same pattern four more times in the past two weeks. Whoever user 669277 was, various painkillers—Demerol, oxycodone, and hydrocodone—were going missing on shifts when he or she was working. Anne wondered how long it had gone on. It would have been hard to notice if you weren't looking for it. Only someone who knew exactly how many pills had been placed into the machine would notice if the count was off, and Anne doubted most of the people who used the machines knew things like that. And only someone who knew which shifts this nurse was working would have thought to look.

Whoever had user ID number 669277 was someone Anne definitely wanted to talk to. Not just about the pill counts being off, either—whoever this person was, they were definitely on the suspect list for the break-in. Now all she had to do was discover who it was. She was pretty sure she could figure that out today once she got to the hospital.

But Anne noticed something else in the records. Maybe it was nothing. There was one doctor whose name seemed to show up more than any of the others. Dr. Vanessa Perez appeared to prescribe Demerol, oxycodone, and fentanyl a lot, in comparison with the other physicians. Anne wasn't sure what—if anything—that meant.

Anne had met Dr. Perez a few times. She worked at an OB/GYN practice right near the hospital, and her patients all delivered their babies at Mercy. She was young, beautiful, and very driven. She wore short skirts and high heels under her lab coats, and she had a long roster of patients. Anne always thought she seemed a bit impersonal, not as warm as some of the doctors, but she had plenty of patients and good health outcomes, so she must be doing something right.

Why was it that her name seemed to come up more often in the records? Did she simply deliver more babies than the other OB/GYNs and therefore have more patients? It was possible. She did seem to be on the Labor and Delivery floor a lot. She could be trying to build up her practice, taking on as many patients as she could. The sheer number of her them could account for the number of pre-scriptions for controlled painkillers she wrote. Or it could be that she performed more C-sections, which typically required more pain medication afterward. Some doctors did lean more heavily on the invasive procedure than others.

Sometimes, the surgical procedure was medically necessary, and it had saved the lives of hundreds of patients and babies, but it also led to more difficult and painful recoveries. It could sometimes be used when it wasn't medically necessary. It was a surgery that could be scheduled, which many doctors—and their patients—found convenient. The hospital's policy was to help as many women as possible have a more natural childbirth experience, but some doctors did end up with more C-sections than others. Was Dr. Perez one of the doctors who relied on the procedure more often? That could account for why her patients were prescribed so many painkillers.

It was also possible she was just freer with the prescription drugs, aiming to keep her patients more comfortable. Or maybe—just maybe—there was more to it than that. She regularly prescribed several of the opioid drugs that had been taken from the Pyxis machine.

Dr. Perez hadn't gone into that recovery room in the time frame when the drugs were taken. Anne knew that for a fact. But did that mean she wasn't tied up in this somehow? Was there any chance there was a reason she prescribed so many painkillers?

Anne looked back at the records again and noticed that Dr. Perez had prescribed the medication that had gone missing after user 669277 had used the machine seven out of eight times in the past few weeks. Was that just coincidence? A result of the seemingly high numbers of prescriptions she wrote? Or was there more to it than that? Was there any chance—Anne knew she was making assumptions here, but she was going to follow her thoughts to their conclusion—that Dr. Perez was writing more prescriptions to give user 669277 an opportunity to get into the machine? Were they working together to gain access to highly controlled substances?

If she was right—if it was true—then either one of them could be addicted to the medicine, or selling the drugs for money, or both. It was a big *if.* And that didn't necessarily prove that Dr. Perez was behind the Pyxis machine break-in. But Anne couldn't dismiss it without at least looking into the possibility. It was still worth looking at Dr. Perez a bit more.

"You're up early."

At least she'd heard Ralph coming this time, so he hadn't scared the blazes out of her like last night. She turned and pushed herself up, and then she leaned in and gave him a kiss as he walked into the kitchen.

"I couldn't sleep."

"I worry you're thinking about this theft too much," Ralph said.

"I think you may be right." Anne lifted the carafe and poured herself another cup of coffee.

"Maybe you should take a break today. Try to focus on other things."

"I wish I could. But it's weighing on me." She added a bit of sugar and a dash of cream, and used her spoon to stir it all up. "Every time I try to think about something else, I just keep coming back to it."

"I'll pray that you find some peace today, in that case." He took a mug down and poured himself coffee too. "Oh, by the way, my car has been making this strange banging sound. I'm going to call Sal to see if he can take a look."

Sal was the mechanic they'd been going to for years. "Is it safe to drive for now? Do you need me to give you a ride?"

"I think it's okay. To me it sounds like something is off with one of the pistons. I need to get it fixed, but it's not unsafe for now. Anyway, I'll call him today and let you know what he says. I'm sure he'll want me to bring the car in, so I'll keep you posted."

"I'd appreciate that." She took a sip of her coffee. "And your prayers."

When Anne arrived at the hospital, she first checked in with Garrison.

"I think user number 669277 has been taking pills from the Pyxis machines," Anne said. "The count is often off after he or she has used the machines."

Garrison blinked. "Wow. Show me."

Anne pulled the binder out from her bag and showed him the pages from the records where she'd noticed the pattern.

"That's some great observation," he said, nodding. "We need to look into that discrepancy and user."

"Do you know who it is?"

"That won't be hard to figure out." Garrison turned back to his computer and pulled up the intranet site and then clicked over to the page where employees managed their hours and benefits. He navigated to a search window, one Anne had never seen before and certainly didn't have access to, and he typed the number into the box at the top. "Miranda Martel," he said. "A nurse."

Anne recognized the name immediately. "She was one of the people that had gone into the recovery room during the window where the theft had occurred."

Garrison was already nodding. "You're right. I'll let the police know right away. Thank you, Anne."

She hesitated. She had told him what she'd come here to let him know, but she also had questions for him.

"Did the police say if there were fingerprints on the ribbon retractor?"

"They didn't find any," Garrison said. "It was clean."

"That makes sense," Anne said. "Half the people in the hospital are wearing disposable gloves at any given time. It wouldn't attract any attention for the thief to have been wearing a pair."

"That's what they think too." Garrison nodded. "I was able to find out the name of the housekeeper who found the retractor in the trash, though."

"Oh? Who was it?"

"It was—" He glanced down at a scribble on a notepad in front of him. "Olga Dotov?"

"Olga." Anne absorbed this news, trying to figure out how it changed things—if it changed things.

"You know her?" Garrison asked.

"She's one of the four people who went into the recovery room in the window when the pills were taken."

"Now that's interesting." He thought for a moment. "If she's the one who broke in, would she then point out the tool that she used?"

"I don't know." It didn't seem to make a lot of sense. "Maybe she wanted to throw suspicion off herself? She thought we wouldn't suspect her if she brought it to our attention?"

"I don't know." Garrison shook his head. Anne would be looking into her more.

The next stop Anne made was the records room. Evelyn was already seated at her computer typing away when Anne walked inside.

"Hi there," Anne said.

"Hey." Evelyn looked up from her screen. "Come here. I want to show you something."

"What did you find?" Anne crossed the room and walked around the desk to peer at Evelyn's screen. She studied a family tree on an online genealogy website.

"I found Joshua Palmer."

It took a minute for Anne to recognize the name. "The soldier?"

"That's right." She pointed at a line, far up on the left side of the tree. "He's right here."

Anne squinted at the screen. Joshua had married Helen Healy in 1859, and their son, Aaron, was born in 1860. There was a line from Aaron showing his marriage to a Beulah Richards in 1881, and they had had three children. "His son survived."

"He did indeed. Little Aaron grew up and got married and had kids of his own. And they grew up and had kids of their own—"

"I think I understand the pattern."

"Until we get all the way here, to this lady. Linda Michaelson. A direct descendant of Joshua, and the creator of this family tree."

"So she would be his..." Anne counted the generations. "She's his great-granddaughter."

"That's right. And she now has grandchildren of her own."

"That's so interesting." Family trees were full of fascinating stories, even if you didn't know any of the people involved. Anne could already spot that Linda's father had had children by several different mothers. Anne wondered what the story was there. And Aaron's daughter Isabelle had lost three daughters in childhood, along with three who survived. There was so much heartbreak, just underneath the lines and dates and names. But for now, she tried to understand what Evelyn was so excited about. "Are you going to reach out to her?"

"I was thinking I would. She seems like she's into family history, so I hope she might be receptive."

"Let me know what you learn."

"I will. Also, I'm planning to go to the South Carolina Historical Society this afternoon to see if I can find Joshua's military records."

"Wasn't he a Union soldier?" Why would they have record of him there?

"Yes, but he was stationed at Fort Sumter before the war, and I've seen records of some of the soldiers. There may not be anything, but I'm interested to see what I can find. Any chance you want to come along?"

The truth was, Anne would. Anne loved the historical society. It might be fun to help Evelyn dig into the records. And it would be a nice break from researching the thief and family vacations.

"Sure. When are you going?"

"I could take my lunch right as you get off work," Evelyn said. "So I could meet you here around two?"

"I'll be here," Anne said. She started to walk toward the door, and then remembered what she'd come in here for in the first place. "Oh, right. I studied the Pyxis record and found a user ID that seemed to be used most often when the pill count was off. It was 669277. Garrison tells me that's Miranda Martel."

Evelyn's eyebrows shot up. "The nurse who went into the recovery room at the right time?"

"That's right. I thought it might be worth checking into her other records to see if there's anything that would be a clue, so I wanted to let you know."

"That's very interesting. I'll take a look."

"Sounds good. And I'll see you at two."

Anne then made her way to Aurora, and Aurora asked her to help with discharge.

Anne had wheeled two patients to the pickup area before she got a text from Shirley. DR. LYLE IS HERE ON THE LABOR AND DELIVERY FLOOR TODAY IF YOU WANT TO TRY TO TALK WITH HIM.

Why, yes. In fact, she did want to try to talk with him. Be RIGHT UP, Anne texted back.

She made her way to the labor and delivery floor and found Shirley at the nurses' station. "I just saw him go in with a patient," Shirley said. "He's down that way."

"I'll just casually stroll in that direction to see if I can 'run into' him," Anne said. A number flashed on the screen behind the nurses' station, calling Shirley to a patient room, and as she got up to check in, Anne began walking down the hallway, the opposite direction of the recovery room. In this area there were more delivery rooms and the nursery, as well as the NICU. Anne stopped in front of the plate-glass window of the nursery and looked at the tiny babies, swaddled tightly. They were so small—it was hard to believe humans could be that small. A nurse held one little guy who was crying, but the others slept peacefully in their bassinets, their squashed little faces calm after their tough fight into the world. Anne remembered gazing at Ariane's face and feeling like she'd never understood love before that moment. She'd been worried she wouldn't be able to love a second child as much, but the moment Lili was born, she had fallen in love all over again.

Footsteps to her right made her turn, but it was just a nurse. Anne wasn't sure what her name was, but she smiled sweetly at Anne as she passed. Anne turned back to the babies. She loved seeing their little faces, plus it also gave her a reason to keep standing here without looking like a crazy person.

A man in a rumpled sweater walked up and peered into the glass. He seemed tired, and he had a day's growth of stubble. She watched as he searched, and then his face lit up. Anne knew what that meant.

"Which one is yours?" Anne asked.

"The one on the end," he said, pointing. "Everett."

"He's beautiful."

"Thank you." The man continued to stare at his son and then took his phone out of his pocket and began to take pictures.

Anne smiled and decided to leave him alone, and she looked up as she heard more footsteps to the right. Ah. There was Dr. Lyle. She stepped away from the window and started to walk down the hallway, trying to seem casual. Then, as she neared him, she feigned surprise.

"Dr. Lyle?" He was thinner than he'd been last time she'd seen him, and he appeared tired. But she still saw the mischievous teenager who'd disrupted her Sunday school class so many Sunday mornings.

He looked at Anne, and then he smiled. "Mrs. Mabry. Good to see you. How are you?"

"I'm all right. How are you? How's Kate?"

"We're good. Kate's great. She's home with our boys these days. We've got two now, can you believe it?"

Anne could believe it, having seen their pictures on his Instagram last night, but she smiled. "How old?"

"Four and two. They're a handful, but we love it."

"I'm so glad." He was probably in his early thirties now, Anne guessed, and had a warm, genuine way of speaking that made her feel like he was really interested in what she had to say.

"Kate's kind of crazy this week because she's taking the boys to see her family out in Ohio this weekend, and trying to pack for a trip with two young kids is nuts, as I'm sure you know. I'm like, flying with two kids on your own? That's Mom of the Year stuff right there."

"For sure." Anne smiled. It took four arms just to carry all the stuff kids needed, never mind corralling the kids themselves. "You're not going with them?"

"I've got to work." He gave a rueful smile. "They've got me scheduled for so many days straight, I don't know that I'll ever get to go on vacation again." He yawned, as if to emphasize his point. "But how about you? How is Reverend Mabry enjoying retirement?"

"Well, he didn't stay retired for all that long."

"That's right! He works here now. I heard that he became a chaplain. How does he like it?"

"It's different than pastoring a church, but he really loves it."

"I'm glad. And how's Lili?"

"She's fine." Anne was a little surprised he remembered Lili. Though they'd both spent a fair amount of time at the church when they were younger, Lili was several years younger than he was. "She was deployed, but she's back home now. She's taking classes toward her degree, and she's raising her daughter. She's doing great."

"I'm glad to hear that." He laughed. "I had such a crush on her when I was in high school. I don't think she even knew who I was, but I definitely paid attention to her."

"Really?" Anne had had no idea. Had Lili known? Would things have worked out any differently if that teen crush had become something more? But there was no use thinking about that now. "That's funny. I'll tell her you said hello."

"I bet she won't even remember me."

Anne would have been inclined to believe this was false modesty—after all, Brendan was smart, successful, and handsome enough that most women would not fail to notice him—but there was something endearingly genuine about his manner that made Anne think it might be real.

"I'll tell her just the same." Anne tried to affect a casual tone as she moved on to what she had come here to say. "I hear there's been a lot of excitement around here these days."

"Oh?" Dr. Lyle cocked his head and wrinkled his brow. "Oh, you mean the Pyxis machine?" She nodded, and he continued. "I did hear about that. It's so crazy. Who would do something like that?"

"I gather the hospital is trying to figure that out."

"The strange thing is, I went into that same room, like, right around the time they think the machine was broken into. I must have been in there just before. I mean, if I'd gone in just a minute or two later, maybe I could have seen what was happening and stopped it."

"You went into the recovery room?" Anne tried to sound surprised, like she'd had no idea.

"I needed to make a quick phone call. Caleb was sick, and I wanted to see whether his fever had broken yet, so I called Kate to check in." He yawned and quickly reached out to cover his mouth before he continued. "The administration doesn't like us to be on the phone in front of patients, and there aren't a lot of good places to make a call out of sight when you're on duty, so when I found the room empty, I ducked inside."

It was what Shirley had suggested. Anne thought back to the security camera footage. Dr. Lyle had been in the delivery room for less than a minute and a half. It was about the right amount of time for a quick phone call to his wife.

"And the machine was the way it should be when you went into the room?"

"I mean, I didn't really look at it, to be honest. But I have to think that if it had been pried open like that, I would have noticed, right?"

"It was pretty hard to miss," Anne admitted. "When I saw it, it was the kind of thing you would definitely notice."

"I only wish I'd come in just a few minutes later so I could have stopped whoever it was."

Anne wished he had too.

"Was Caleb okay?"

"He was resting peacefully, and he's doing much better. Just some kind of summer stomach bug. He's already back to his normal crazy self, which means they don't have to change their travel plans."

"I'm glad to hear it."

Just then he looked down at his beeping cell phone that was hooked to the pocket of his lab coat. "I'm sorry, I've got to run. But it was great seeing you. Say hi to Reverend Mabry for me."

"I will," she said to his back, as he was already retreating down the hallway. She thought about the conversation as she headed toward the nurses' station. If the machine had been intact when Brendan had gone into the recovery room, that meant Miranda Martel hadn't been the one to break into it. It would have had to have been either Luke or Olga, as they were the only two who had gone into the room after him. But was it possible it had been broken, and he hadn't noticed? If he was distracted by his phone and his sick child, she could see how it was possible he had missed it, as obvious as it seemed.

Which meant that Anne wasn't a lot closer to knowing what had really happened. She doubted Brendan—Dr. Lyle, she was supposed to call him now—had done it, but any of the other three could have.

Anne glanced at the clock. She should head back toward the second floor to see if there were any more patients who needed help getting down to the discharge area, but she had time to make a quick phone call first. She ducked into an empty postpartum room and pulled out her phone. She scrolled through the names until she found the one she was looking for. Nick. She called, and the phone rang once, twice, three times, before it went straight to voice mail.

"Hi, Nick, it's Anne, just checking in to see how you're doing. Give me a call when you get a chance."

She hung up and stared down at her phone. Was that even Nick's number anymore? Did he still have his phone? She didn't know. *Take care of him, Lord,* she prayed, and then she tucked her phone back into her pocket and stepped out into the hallway.

Chapter Seven

AFTER ANNE LEFT THE LABOR and Delivery floor, she headed downstairs and went to the gift shop. Joy was behind the counter, ringing up a line of customers, and Anne browsed the rack of greeting cards while she waited for Joy to be free. Once Joy had taken care of her customers, Anne approached the counter.

"It's Miranda Martel."

"What is?"

"The nurse who has been stealing drugs from the Pyxis machines. The one Evelyn and Shirley knew about but wouldn't tell us the name of."

"How do you know?"

Anne explained how she'd looked through the records and searched the ID number for the nurse whose counts were consistently off.

"So you think she's been skimming drugs from the machines."

"It's very possible."

"Huh." Joy nodded, and seemed to be thinking it through. "She was the first person who went into the room in that security camera footage, though, right?"

Anne could guess the problem Joy was about to point out. "She was the first person in there after the patient went out."

"If she was the one who broke into the machine, all three of the other people who went after her didn't notice the machine was broken," Joy said.

"Or they did but didn't say anything."

"If we were talking about one person not noticing, that would be easier to believe. But all three?"

"You're right." Anne thought through this, trying to understand how the pieces all fit together. "And Doctor Lyle said he didn't notice it open when he went in—"

"When did you talk to Dr. Lyle?"

Anne explained how she'd spoken to him just a little while ago. "He didn't think the machine was broken when he went in to call his wife, but he also admitted he wasn't really looking, so maybe he missed it."

"And maybe Luke and Olga also missed it?" Joy cocked her head. "And yet it was obvious enough that you saw it while walking past the room in the hallway?"

"It's possible," Anne said, but it sounded thin. "Okay, that's a problem we need to figure out. But we know Miranda is stealing drugs, and that she works on the L&D floor, and she went into the recovery room at the right time. How could it not be her who broke into the machine?"

"We don't know for sure she's stealing drugs," Joy said. "We know the pill count is sometimes off after she uses the Pyxis machine. Maybe she's just not especially exact in her counting. We have to keep all possibilities open for now."

"I guess. But...okay. She's highly suspected of stealing drugs. And then the drugs she's suspected to have stolen were taken when the machine was broken into. How can there not be a connection?"

"I'm not saying there's not. I'm just saying, let's not jump to any conclusions. There might be other possibilities we haven't seen that we'd miss if we just make assumptions."

"Fine." Anne could acknowledge that Joy was right here. "Point taken."

"I'm not saying it's not her. Just trying to cover all the bases." Joy leaned forward, resting her arms on the counter. "So let's say Miranda has been stealing medication. And let's say it was Miranda who broke into the machine. Let's say Dr. Lyle was mistaken, and the machine was open when he came in and he didn't notice. Why would Miranda change tactics?"

"What do you mean?"

"Say she has been stealing pills, just a few here and a few there, but not enough that anyone could prove it. Why would she now break into the machine if what she's been doing so far has been working?"

"Something must have changed on her end." Anne tried to think about what. "Maybe she suddenly needed more than just a few pills here and there."

"Maybe. But why?"

"I don't know." Anne felt deflated, realizing how many holes her theory had.

"If the hospital didn't know who was recording the count wrong until this morning, they wouldn't have had time to confront her yet."

"And if they haven't confronted her, and she doesn't know they suspect her, it doesn't make a lot of sense for her to suddenly change her tactic," Anne admitted. "But Shirley knew they were trying to figure out who it was that was messing up the count so often. If Shirley knew, Miranda probably knew as well. Maybe she knew her time was running out, and the hospital would figure out it was her eventually. Maybe she got desperate enough to break in while she could."

"It's possible. It's conjecture, but it's possible."

"Or maybe there's another reason for her to change tactics," Anne said. "What would she be doing with all these pills anyway?"

"Taking them, I assume," Joy said. "She wouldn't be the first nurse to become addicted to painkillers."

"That's the most logical answer. But what if there was a different reason?" Anne asked.

Joy's brow wrinkled. "Like what?"

"I found something else interesting in the Pyxis machine records," Anne said. She explained how she'd seen Dr. Vanessa Perez's name come up in the records more than anyone else's.

"So you think Dr. Perez is writing more prescriptions than necessary, and that's giving Miranda an opportunity to use the machine more often and take an extra pill here and there?"

Anne nodded.

"And then what? Does she give them to Dr. Perez?"

"I think so."

"And then what?"

"Maybe she takes them? Or maybe she sells them, and they split the profit."

Joy pressed her lips together, and seemed to be considering. "Dr. Perez couldn't get into the machine herself, is what you're thinking. Doctors can write the prescriptions, but they don't have access to the Pyxis machines themselves."

"That's right," Anne said. "You have to use your fingerprint to log in, along with your ID card. So she could prescribe medication all she wanted, but she couldn't get it from the machine without help."

"And if the doctor wanted to get her hands on some oxycodone and hydrocodone, she might make a deal with someone who did have access—say, a nurse—and pay her to get the medication."

"That's my theory, anyway."

"And if Miranda worried she was about to get caught, if she knew the hospital had noticed discrepancies in the records—"

"It's possible she decided to go big and make one last sale before they put a stop to it for good."

Joy nodded, her expression thoughtful. "Do we know if Dr. Perez was on the L&D floor the day of the theft?"

"She was," Anne said. "She prescribed several doses of Demerol that afternoon."

"So even though Dr. Perez never entered the recovery room where the machine was broken into, it's possible she was the one actually behind the theft."

"I'm just saying it's a possibility."

"If it's true—and it's a big *if*—"

Anne nodded, acknowledging the truth of Joy's words.

"If you're right, then we need to find a way to talk to Dr. Perez."

"I was thinking the same thing."

"Do you know if she's at the hospital today?"

"Based on the Pyxis records, it seems like she's usually seeing patients at her office on Wednesdays. I guess you never know if she might get called to the hospital, but I think most OB/GYN practices usually have a doctor on call at the hospital while the others work out of the office."

"Hmm." Joy pushed herself up from her elbows. "So we'd need to get in to her office to see her." Then she laughed.

"What?"

"I was just thinking of excuses to make an appointment with her." She gave Anne a wry grin. "Do you think she'd believe one of is having a baby?"

Anne laughed too. "I highly doubt it. Medicine has advanced a lot, but it's not *that* advanced."

"I didn't think so." She shrugged. "Well, I guess we'll just have to find another way to get in to talk to her. Lacy will be here soon. How does leaving in half an hour sound?"

"I'll be waiting for you."

Thirty minutes later, they had walked the short distance to Albemarle OB/GYN. The office was on the third floor of a modern medical building housed in a nineteenth-century warehouse, and the lobby and hallways had big, airy windows that let in lots of sunlight. They found the office and stepped inside the waiting area filled with patients in padded chairs, but the big windows along the side wall made the space feel bright. Anne marched up to the desk, and a woman looked up from her computer and smiled.

"Hi there. Checking in?" She was young, maybe midtwenties, with artificially blond hair and wide green eyes.

"I'm not actually a patient," Anne said. "My friend and I are working with Mercy Hospital, and we had a few questions for Dr. Perez."

"Okay..." Her cheery voice faltered for a moment. "Do you have an appointment?"

"No, we don't. But we were hoping Dr. Perez might have a moment between patients to speak with us," Joy said, coming up beside Anne. The receptionist looked from Anne to Joy and back again, confused.

"It's very important," Anne added. "It's about an incident at the hospital."

"Okay...," she said uncertainly. "Why don't you have a seat, and I'll see if Dr. Perez can spare a moment?"

"Thank you."

After Anne and Joy found two seats next to each other, the receptionist picked up the phone and talked softly into it. Anne looked around the room. Women in various stages of pregnancy sat around the room, along with a few uncomfortable-looking men. A soap opera played quietly on the television in the corner of the room. Most of the patients looked down at their phones. Anne picked up a magazine from the table next to her chair. THE PERFECT NAME FOR YOUR BABY IS OUT THERE! One headline read. ARE YOU GETTING ENOUGH VITAMINS? HOW TO TELL, read another. CHOOSING THE RIGHT STROLLER. POSITIVE DISCIPLINE THAT REALLY WORKS. STAYING SLIM THROUGHOUT YOUR PREGNANCY. Goodness. There was so much pressure on moms. Did people really worry about looking slim in their ninth month or think there was a "perfect" name or "right" stroller?

She turned and saw that Joy was looking at a seed company's website on her phone. "Doing some shopping?"

"I was thinking of planting some different colors of iris this fall. I'm checking to see what bulbs they had in stock."

"Ah." That was a better use of time than sitting here reading magazines that didn't apply to her. Anne would use this time to do some research too. She pulled out her own phone and opened up an app that allowed you to book houses and apartments all over the world and tried to figure out how to search for mountain cabins. But the app's front page had an ad for a business called Unique Stays, with a picture of a floating houseboat on it. Interesting. Anne tapped on that, and she was taken to a page of unusual homes she could rent in the area. There was an ad for a full-fledged tree house, complete with a bathroom and two bedrooms. Now that could be fun. It reminded her of the old movie *Swiss Family Robinson* she'd loved when she was a kid. Here was a place where they could stay in a yurt. There were also several tiny houses in various picturesque settings—but why would she want to squish her whole family into 150 square feet for a week? And here was an actual tower you could rent, sleeping in the top of the tower overlooking the mountains. Addie would feel like Rapunzel in that place. But Anne couldn't see staying there for a week. There were a couple of glamping sites—camping, but with a bed and running water?—and a geodesic dome, and—

"Ms. Mabry?"

Anne looked up as a nurse in a white coat appeared in the open doorway that led to the back.

"The doctor will see you now."

Anne stood up quickly, and Joy rose next to her, and they followed the nurse down the hall and into a small exam room. Joy plopped herself down on the exam table, the paper crinkling beneath her, while Anne sat in a chair at the side of the room.

"You're just—you're just here to speak with the doctor?" She held a paper exam robe in her hands, looking from one to the other.

"That's right," Anne said. "We won't be needing a robe."

The woman nodded, still seeming confused, and then stepped out and closed the door behind her.

"It's been a while since I've been in a room like this," Joy said, gesturing at the ultrasound machine in the corner. The walls were hung with Dr. Perez's framed degrees and photos of smiling newborns in cabbage leaves and perched on pumpkins. Anne nodded. She'd accompanied Lili on most of her prenatal doctor's visits, since Matt hadn't really been interested in seeing his daughter develop in the womb—or out of it, as it turned out.

"What do you think all these buttons do?" Joy leaned over to the machine and looked down at it.

"I don't think you should touch that," Anne started to say just as the door opened and Dr. Perez entered the room. She wore stiletto heels and a chic pencil shirt and silk blouse under her lab coat.

"Ms. Mabry?" She looked up from a clipboard at Anne, and then at Joy.

"That's me."

"I'm told you wanted to talk to me?"

"That's right. We're working with Mercy Hospital, and we were hoping we could discuss an incident at the hospital on Monday," Anne said.

"Okay…" She let her voice trail off. "Is this about that machine again?"

"Again?"

"The police already came to see me," Dr. Perez said. "And I already told them that yes, I was there on the floor, but I was delivering a baby when those drugs were taken. I don't have access to those machines and don't have the first clue about how to work them even if I did. And I certainly didn't take a crowbar to the machine."

Another person who assumed it had been a crowbar, Anne noted. Where did they think a crowbar had been hiding on the labor and delivery floor? How would the thief have carried a crowbar down the hall without anyone noticing?

"You write prescriptions that are filled by nurses who use the machines, right?" Joy asked.

"Yeah?" She crossed her arms over her chest. What was she so defensive about if she had nothing to hide?

"How do you decide which drugs to prescribe to your patients?" Anne asked.

"Are you serious right now?"

Anne nodded, and she waited. She knew there was power in her silence. Many people couldn't handle it and would rush to fill the quiet.

"I prescribe medication based on who needs what. I follow all state and federal guidelines about dosage. Who are you, the prescription police?"

"Do you know which nurse fills the prescriptions?"

"Some of them. Why?"

"Do you know a nurse named Miranda Martel?"

"I don't think so. I don't really know a lot of their names."

She caught Joy's eye. Dr. Perez worked with the nurses several times a week, and she hadn't bothered to learn their names?

"Is she the one who broke into that machine?" Dr. Perez asked.

"She has brown hair? Shoulder length?" Anne tried.

Dr. Perez shook her head. "There are dozens of nurses there. That could be any of them."

It could be a handful of them, Anne thought. But more importantly, she couldn't tell if Dr. Perez really didn't know who Miranda was or if she was pretending not to.

"What happens to the medication that doesn't get used?" Anne asked.

"What, like, if a patient doesn't take it all?" Her eyes narrowed. "Why wouldn't they take the medication? These women have just been through major physical trauma, especially those who've had C-sections. They are in serious pain. I write prescriptions that can help with that. Why wouldn't they take it?"

She looked an Anne like she was crazy. Anne wanted to ask about why she wrote so many more prescriptions than the other doctors, but before she could get the words out, Dr. Perez said, "I need to get back to work. I have a waiting room full of patients. If you police people are going to come in here again asking questions about things I don't know anything about, please make an appointment. I need to put my patients first."

With that, she turned and walked out the door. Anne waited until the door closed behind her before she faced Joy. "Did she just say she thought we were with the police?"

Joy giggled. "That's what it sounded like."

"I guess that must have been why she bothered to speak with us at all. My guess is she wouldn't have unless she thought she had to."

"It also means she's never noticed either one of us, even though we're at the hospital every day."

"Maybe that gives credence to her claim that she doesn't know who any of the nurses are," Anne said, thinking.

"In any case, she wasn't especially forthcoming," Joy added.

"Either that or she genuinely doesn't know anything," Anne said.

"I suppose it's hard to guess."

A knock came at the door, and the nurse who had led them to the room popped her head in. "If you're done in here, could you kindly make your way to the front so we can bring another patient in here?"

They were being kicked out.

Chapter Eight

JOY AND ANNE HEADED BACK to the hospital, and when they were approaching the building, Anne spotted something in the Grove, the outdoor green space that was nestled between the old and new wings of the hospital. "You head on up. I'm going to stop and talk to someone," Anne said to Joy.

Joy went inside the building, and Anne walked out into the grassy garden. A stiff breeze whipped in off the harbor, making the area cooler, even at this time of year, though the humidity out here still made her feel like she'd walked into a sauna. Anne followed the path that cut through the grassy median and glanced at the angel statue on her left, near what used to be the front entrance to the historic wing. The angel's familiar presence was comforting, every single time she saw it.

Anne followed the path down toward the tables under the magnolia trees, trying to affect a careless attitude, and…there she was. Sitting alone at a picnic table in the shade, staring at her phone. Crushed shells crunched under her feet as Anne walked toward her. Approaching, she pretended to be absorbed in the blooming hibiscus and rose of Sharon bushes that ran along one side of the path.

"Hi, Anne," Miranda said. She set her cell phone down and looked up at her.

"Miranda." Anne put on her widest smile. Should she pretend she hadn't seen her there? Was it too obvious she had? "Hello."

"Did you come looking for me?"

Anne hesitated.

"I figured you'd come find me soon. I've heard that you were talking to people who were around on Monday at the time that Pyxis machine was broken into. I wondered when you'd get to me."

Where had she heard that? People were talking about her questions? Oh dear. Garrison wasn't going to be happy about that. Miranda grinned, but there was something in her face that Anne couldn't read. Anne tried not to let it get under her skin.

"In that case, I guess you know I found the machine broken into and am trying to make sense of what I saw that day."

The crust of a cheese sandwich, the edges of the yellow cheese turned up and dewy in the humidity, sat on a napkin on the table in front of Miranda. A half-eaten serving of yogurt sat next to it. A bee buzzed around the container, but she swatted it away.

"Well, I'm happy to answer whatever questions you had. I really hope they find whoever did this."

"I do too," Anne said. Miranda's directness had thrown her off, and she tried to recover her equanimity. "I guess in that case, maybe you could tell me what you remember about Monday, from say eleven to twelve thirty or so." Anne already knew that Miranda had gone into the recovery room at 11:48, nearly forty-five minutes before Anne had discovered the machine broken into, and knew from the Pyxis records she'd verified this morning that Miranda had retrieved a prescription for hydrocodone from the machine at that point, but she wanted to see what Miranda said about it.

"Sure thing. I was assigned to half a dozen patients in the post-partum rooms. Most were doing fine, but there was one woman who was in a lot of pain. Tara, I think her name was. She'd had an emergency C-section after a long labor, and she was whimpering a lot. She needed more pain meds."

"What do you do, in that case? When a patient needs medication?"

"We can't just hand out drugs, obviously, though sometimes I wish we could. We're the ones there with the patients and can see what they need. But only doctors can prescribe them, and we hand them out once the doctor has written the prescription and the pharmacy has entered it into the Pyxis system. So if there's any left in what she's already been prescribed, I'll get her that. In this case, there wasn't anything left, so I contacted Dr. Perez and asked her to refill the patient's prescription for hydrocodone so I could give her more."

"Did she refill it?"

"Yeah, she's good about that."

"Does that happen often? That you reach out to a specific doctor?"

"Depends. Some doctors are more stingy with the drugs. That's hard, because they're not around to see their patients suffering. It's like they forget what major trauma childbirth is and how much pain even the smoothest birth causes. So we just have to get by with Tylenol and do our best to make them comfortable. But some doctors are fine with it. Dr. Perez is good about making sure her patients are comfortable."

There was probably a good reason some doctors were more careful about handing out addictive painkillers. But Dr. Perez was more free with them; Anne knew that from the machine's records. She just needed to find out if there was a reason beyond care for her patients that drove the doctor.

"Do you contact Dr. Perez a lot?"

"I mean, she has a lot of patients, so yes, probably more than some others, but I wouldn't say it's an especially lot."

And yet Dr. Perez had said she didn't know who Miranda was. Was there a connection between them? Anne couldn't tell if one of them was lying or not. On the table, the screen of Miranda's phone lit up. The name CRESTVIEW appeared, though Anne was reading it upside down. She must have had it on silent. Miranda reached over and touched a button on the side of the phone to decline the call.

"Does a patient ever not need the full amount of a drug that's been prescribed?" Anne asked, changing direction a little.

"Sometimes they refuse it, sure. But that's rare. After major abdominal surgery like that, most need the relief."

"What happens to the medication if a patient doesn't take it?" Anne asked.

"There's a bin we put it in," Miranda said. "It's locked, so no one can get at the medication once it's in there."

"Do people ever not return unused medication to the bin?"

Miranda narrowed her eyes and leaned forward just a bit. "Not that I know of." She waved her hand again, swatting the bee away. "I mean, it probably does happen, but I haven't heard of it."

Anne wasn't sure she believed her, knowing what she knew about the discrepancies in the records, but Miranda appeared to be earnest and open. Anne needed to push ahead.

"Let's go back to Monday. You were taking care of the patients, and then what?"

"Well, around eleven forty-five, I went into the C-section recovery room to see if the prescription I'd requested for Tara had come through. But you already know that, right?"

Once again, Anne was flustered, but Miranda smiled.

"I assume you saw the security camera footage, and that's why you're talking to me."

"Have you seen the footage?" How did she know what was on it?

"No, but I mean, obviously there's a camera in the hallway. I know I went into that room in the window the police think someone broke into that machine. I know having been in that room makes me a suspect. But I didn't do it, so I'm trying to be as helpful as I can so the hospital can find the person who did."

"Fair enough." Anne took a breath, trying to stay on top of this. "Did you see anything unusual about the machine when you went in?"

"You mean, did I notice that several of the drawers had been pried open?" She smiled, her eyes twinkling. "No, I did not. Everything looked normal."

That wasn't exactly what Anne had meant, though. She knew the machine hadn't been broken before Miranda had gone inside. She wanted to know if Miranda had broken into it herself. But how could she come out and ask that?

"And it looked normal when I left the room too," Miranda added. "The drawers were closed, and the system had reset. It looked just like it should."

"Had the prescription for Tara been entered?" Anne asked.

"Yes, so I logged in and took two hydrocodone, and then I gave them to her."

"You gave them both to her?"

For the first time, Miranda's face revealed something other than friendliness. "Of course. What else would I do with the pills?"

What else indeed.

"What did you do after that?"

Miranda's phone lit up with the name Crestview again. She silenced it like last time.

"Well, it was time for my lunch break, so I checked in at the nurses' station, and then I went to the break room to grab my lunch and came out here. I eat in the Grove pretty much every day, unless it's raining."

"It is nice." It felt like she was wrapped in a wet blanket. "You don't mind the humidity?"

"I'm always freezing inside the hospital. I come outside to warm up." She was making a joke, Anne could see that, but Anne wondered if there was another layer she wasn't getting. It *was* uncommonly cold inside the hospital, which was why she always wore a sweater.

Miranda glanced down at her phone again, and Anne followed her gaze. There were two notifications about the missed calls from Crestview.

"I'm sorry, but my lunch is almost over, and I need to make a quick phone call before I head back in. Is there anything else I can help you with?"

Anne couldn't think of more questions to ask her. She had already denied breaking into the machine or pocketing extra pills. Anne wasn't convinced she didn't have something to do with this theft, but Miranda had covered all her bases.

"Will you let me know if you think of anything that might be relevant?" Anne asked.

"Of course." Miranda began packing up her garbage and stood up. "Like I said, I want whoever did this to be caught as much as you do. In fact, is there anything I can do? Maybe join you in talking to people? I know you have a reputation for solving mysteries, but maybe I can help?"

"Thank you." Once again, Anne wasn't sure what to say. "I'll let you know."

Anne didn't want to leave, wasn't convinced there wasn't more to learn, but she couldn't exactly just stand here. She turned and headed toward the hospital. She glanced behind her just before she went inside the doors and saw that Miranda was holding the phone up to her ear, talking. Anne left feeling unsettled. Miranda had been nothing but earnest and open. And yet Anne couldn't help feeling that she was hiding something. Maybe it was just that she was skimming medication from the machines on a regular basis and was being overly helpful here to throw suspicion off herself. But maybe there was more to it than that.

Anne shook her head as she pushed open the glass door, and a wave of cold air hit her as she stepped inside. It was blessedly cool in here. But as soon as she entered, someone started walking toward her.

"I hear you were asking about me at the club." It was Luke Merritt, and he walked right up to her and stopped directly in front of her. Had he been waiting for her? He seemed to have been.

"Oh. Hello." She took a step back to put some space between them, but Luke just stepped forward again. He really was very large when he was this close, Anne realized.

"You have some nerve, you know that? Did you think it wasn't going to get back to me? I've known Leo and Harry for years. They called as soon as you left, told me some nosy old lady from the hospital was asking about whether I was stealing drugs to sell at the club. I knew right away who they were talking about."

Anne wanted to dispute the "old" part but knew better than to argue with him just then.

"Let me be clear about this," he continued. He blinked rapidly. "I don't do drugs, and I never have. I don't sell drugs either, and I never would. I had nothing to do with that theft Monday. I didn't take those drugs."

"You were in the recovery room alone with the Pyxis machine for three minutes." Anne tried to keep her voice calm and level. "What were you doing in there that whole time?"

On some level, she knew it was dangerous to be antagonizing him. He was big—much bigger than she was—and very strong. He was clearly trying to use his size to intimidate her right now. But she was in a crowded hospital, and people walked back and forth through these doors all the time. He might threaten her, but he wouldn't hurt her, not here. Plus, she knew this might be her only chance to get answers from him.

"It's none of your business, but you know what? I'm sick of you asking questions, so I'm going to go ahead and tell you so you'll just leave me alone." He cracked the knuckles on his right hand and kept blinking. It was unsettling, even if he couldn't help it. "I was checking my stocks."

"What?" Anne couldn't have heard him right.

"On my phone. We're not supposed to be seen using our phones on the floors while we're at work, so I ducked into the recovery room because no one was there. Everyone does it. You go into any unoccupied room in this hospital, and there are employees in there on their phones." Shirley had said the same thing, and Dr. Lyle as well, and in Anne's experience, it was often true. She'd done is herself just yesterday.

"You were checking your stocks on your phone?"

"Yeah. I have an app."

That wasn't the part that had confused Anne. She wouldn't have guessed—she wouldn't have assumed—

"What, you don't believe me? You want to see it?" He stepped back a bit and pulled out his phone and punched in a code, and then he pulled up an app for a stock brokerage Anne recognized.

"Do you do a lot of investing?" Anne asked. Ralph had a pension from his time at St. Michael's, and they had managed to put aside a little in an IRA over the years, but she had never paid much attention to the stock market, and she was surprised to find out that Luke did. Maybe she shouldn't have been, but there it was.

"Sure. A bunch of buddies and I are part of a Reddit group that shares about hot stock tips. I started with a little bit of cash and have grown it into a pretty nice chunk of change. Not enough to retire on yet, but I'm working on it."

"So…you went into the recovery room to check in on it?"

Anne figured Ralph probably looked into their investments once a year or so. She couldn't imagine him ever ducking into an empty room during a shift to check out their portfolio.

"Just that morning, I'd bought some seriously devalued stock for a company that just filed bankruptcy. A movie theater chain. Who goes to movie theaters anymore? But I'm banking on a rebound once they consolidate their debt, so I wanted to see if the number had moved."

"And…" Anne didn't even know what to ask. "Had it?"

"No, it had gone down, so I bought more shares."

Anne didn't follow his logic, but maybe that was why she wasn't a millionaire yet. "You did all that in the recovery room?"

"Yes. And then I put my phone away and walked back out and took the wheelchairs down, like I'd been sent to do."

The story was so bizarre, so implausible, that it almost seemed like it had to be true. Who would make up something like that? But she still had some questions.

"You said you've never done drugs."

"It's true. Early on in my time at Shade, I saw an overdose, and that was it for me. Watching him slip away like that, seeing that all his friends were too afraid of getting caught themselves to get him the help he needed—no way. It's happening so often these days too. No thanks. Not for me."

"But what about your arrest? You served time for possession."

Luke let out a noise that was somewhere between a grunt and a whine. "What are you, a stalker?"

"It wasn't hard to find that with a simple Google search."

He let out an expletive. "I'll tell you about that, not that's it's any of your business, it if means you'll leave me alone."

Anne didn't ever want to be this close to this man again, but she wasn't going to commit to that, not yet, so she stayed silent and waited for him to go on.

"My girlfriend worked at Shade too. A cocktail waitress. Like I said, I never did drugs, but sure, they were always around. The cops musta heard about that, so they did a raid one night. My girlfriend had some smack on her." Anne recognized the street name for heroin, a close relative of the opioids like oxycodone and hydrocodone. "She started to freak when they busted in. She was going to lose custody of her kids if she got caught again. So I took the pills. I took the fall. She got to keep her kids. I went to prison. She found a new guy while I was locked away. End of story."

"You expect me to believe that you were just holding the drugs for someone else?" It was the oldest excuse in the book; even Anne knew that.

"Believe what you want." He shrugged. "It's the truth."

Anne wasn't sure of his story. It sounded ridiculous. And yet when he said it, it seemed like it could actually be true. "And then once you got out of prison, you went back to working at the club?"

"I needed money, didn't I?" His blinking had slowed down but now it started up again. "I didn't stay long, though. I started looking around. I wanted something more stable, with better hours and benefits. It sounded nice to have medical insurance, you know?"

Somehow over the course of the conversation, the anger seemed to have drained out of him, and he didn't seem as threatening as he had just a few minutes ago.

"And how long have you been working at Mercy?"

"Almost three months. I'm still in my probation period. And if I get fired for this, I won't get any of my benefits."

Anne almost felt bad for him. Almost. "When you went into the recovery room on Monday, did you see the Pyxis machine?"

"I didn't even know what those machines were called or what they were for until people started accusing me of breaking into one. No, I didn't see it. Or, I mean, I guess I probably saw it, but it was like furniture, you know? Not something I paid any attention to."

"Did you see the ribbon retractor?" Anne threw it out as a test.

"The what?" He shook his head. "I didn't see no ribbon."

He could have been lying, she knew. But she didn't think he was.

Anne didn't want to write Luke off entirely, but standing here talking to him now, she found that she kind of believed him. Sure, he could be lying, and he had not only a clear motive but also a drug arrest in his past. But for whatever reason, Luke didn't look so big and intimidating any longer, and Anne found she didn't really think he had done it.

Which left her even more confused than ever.

Chapter Nine

ANNE MET EVELYN IN HER office just after two, and then they both drove their cars over to the South Carolina Historical Society's archives, which were housed on the second floor of the College of Charleston's Addlestone Library. They walked up the stairs and through the glass doors and signed in at the desk. Evelyn told the receptionist what they were looking for, and she told them to have a seat at one of the tables and promised she would bring them what they needed shortly. Evelyn led Anne to one of the long wooden tables, and they took two seats next to each other. The room was lined on two sides by tall bookshelves, and the only other patrons were hunched over an old plat map on the far side of the room.

"These are all the military records we have from that period." She set four thick, heavy books down on the table. "I'm going to need to ask you to wear these as you handle the records." She also set out two pairs of white cotton gloves.

"Of course," Evelyn said, reaching for the gloves. "Thank you so much."

"Please let me know if you need anything," the archivist said before turning back toward the desk.

They slipped the gloves on, and Evelyn pulled the books close. She pushed one toward Anne and took the top one for herself.

"What are we looking for exactly?" Anne asked, opening the cover. Inside were hundreds of plastic sleeves, each containing a sheet of yellowed paper. The top page in this book seemed to be a list of supplies requisitioned to Castle Pinckney—another fort just off the coast of Charleston—when it was used as a military prison after the first Battle of Bull Run.

"Records of soldiers injured and killed," Evelyn said. "I'm looking for any record that Joshua's family was given word of his death, or anything related to his time at Mercy."

"All right." It seemed like a long shot to Anne, but she was happy enough to look through interesting files.

Behind the requisition list was a record of the names of the Confederate soldiers who had fought the Great Fire of 1861, lit as part of General Sherman's bloody march to the sea. Huge swaths of Charleston had burned, destroying many of its most famous landmarks, including several churches and civic buildings. Mercy Hospital itself had mostly burned to the ground. What was now known as the historic wing was the only part of the original structure that had survived the fire. It was one of the saddest days in the proud city's history. But Anne scanned the names of the soldiers who had fought the fire, and she didn't see any reference to Joshua or even any Union troops at all.

Anne flipped through the plastic sleeves, trying to make sense of all the different scraps of information they held. She found a letter from General James Archer to Confederate president Jefferson Davis, recounting his time as a prisoner of war after being captured at Gettysburg. She found the transcript of a sermon preached by the rector at the French Huguenot church calling for the people of the congregation to seek the Lord's will and pray for peace. But she didn't find anything about Joshua Palmer, or about Mercy Hospital.

After Anne made it through the first book, she closed it and then leaned back and stretched. She hadn't realized how much she'd been hunched over the pages. "I think I'll take a quick break," she said. Evelyn nodded but didn't look up. She could examine documents for hours on end. Anne might not make it as long as Evelyn did here, but that was why they'd brought two cars. Anne made her way out of the room, back down the stairs, and out onto the street. She checked her phone, but there were no messages. Still nothing from Nick. She walked to the corner and back, stretched her arms up over her head, and then returned to the archives.

"I found it," Evelyn said in a loud whisper as soon as Anne sat down.

"You found what?"

"Records from Fort Sumter. The official count of the Union troops that were stationed there. Joshua Palmer is listed as Missing."

"Missing?"

"As in, they didn't know what happened to him."

"How did they not know what happened to him, though? Someone obviously transported him to the hospital."

"I don't presume to judge the record-keeping skills of soldiers in battle. I imagine it must have been chaotic and frightening, and keeping accurate records was probably not the first thing on people's minds."

"Fair enough." Anne could see that Evelyn was excited about what she'd found, but Anne wasn't quite sure why. "So what does that mean?"

"Maybe nothing," Evelyn said. She must have seen Anne's face fall, because she quickly added, "But it does mean that we have reason to believe Joshua's family never knew what happened to him. If the army didn't know, and his letters were never sent, it's possible they never received word about his fate."

"And…" Why was Evelyn grinning like that? "Why is that a good thing?"

"Oh, it's not a good thing." Evelyn shook her head. "I mean, if I'm right, think about what his poor wife must have gone through, never learning what happened to her husband. Think about his mother, and his son. How awful to just never know. To hope that one day he might come walking back down the road, tired and hungry and thin, but alive. And the whole time he was buried in some mass grave in South Carolina."

"Is that what happened to him?"

"I imagine so. It's the most likely scenario, anyway."

"Goodness."

"But do you see what this means?"

"Not really," Anne admitted.

"We may have the chance to finally let a family know what happened to their long-lost ancestor."

That night after dinner, Anne was determined to make a decision about their family vacation. It was only a few weeks away, and she needed to make plans. She had had an idea while she was cooking, and now she wanted to see if it was reasonable.

Anne opened up a browser window and typed in HOTELS NIAG-
ARA FALLS. Her parents had taken the family to see the famous waterfall on a road trip to visit her maternal grandparents in Michigan
when Anne was probably around ten. She had been blown away by its
power and beauty. She still remembered the roar of the water and the
feel of the spray as she stood on the top deck of the *Maid of the Mist*,
bouncing in the waves at the base of the falls. It had been one of the
first times she remembered being totally awed by God's creation, and
now she wondered if she could share that feeling with Addie. Plus, she
remembered the town of Niagara Falls as a fun vacation spot, with
lots of activities for families.

She saw that the hotels overlooking Horseshoe Falls were all on
the Canadian side of the border, and Anne was pretty sure her pass-
port was expired. There wasn't much chance she could get a new one
before they had to leave. But on the New York side, there were many
places that were close to the state park. Here was one on the eighth
floor of a hotel, overlooking the park and the rapids that led up to
the American Falls. That was beautiful. But it was pricey. There
were more modest options farther from the falls, though. That
would be okay.

They could drive to New York from Charleston with a stopover
along the way. She pulled up a map and looked up what was halfway. Ooh, they could stop in West Virginia and see the Blue Ridge
Mountains. They were supposed to be beautiful. And then, after
they toured Niagara Falls, maybe they could head west to Yellow-
stone. Anne had never seen Old Faithful. That was it. They'd do a
road trip and see the highlights of American landscape. Maybe
they could keep going to the Grand Canyon, and Joshua Tree. But

it would take several days to drive that far. And then the Grand Canyon…yikes. Anne started to calculate the number of days on the road, and she quickly realized that this plan was not feasible. They would spend far more time in the car than actually seeing the sights.

She sat back and rubbed her eyes. She should probably just go back to the original plan and find a place by the beach. There had to be a decent house out there. She would look again.

But an hour later, she was bleary-eyed and more frustrated than ever. Was she ever going to find a place? And why was it all on her, anyway? There were three adults in this scenario, so why was she the one doing all the work, trying to come up with a plan? Maybe she should tell Ralph and Lili she wanted them to not just brainstorm ideas but do some research to see if they were at all feasible. Maybe she should…

What she needed to do was take a break. She was getting too worked up and was in no state to talk to anyone at the moment. She knew it was silly to get so frustrated about a vacation. She just wanted everything to be perfect. She wanted to make memories that would last a lifetime. But if she wasn't careful, the memories they all had of this time would be of Anne having a temper tantrum. She closed out of all the travel planning websites. She would try again in the morning, after she'd had some rest.

What she should do was close her laptop and go get ready for bed. She'd make herself a cup of tea first, though. She pushed herself up and filled the kettle, and while the water heated, she selected a nice chamomile tea bag. She set the bag in her favorite mug, poured hot water over it, and watched the steam rise as it steeped. This was what she needed. This was comforting.

The only problem was, now that she'd forced herself to stop thinking about vacation planning, her mind had gone back to missing drugs, circling around what could have happened to them. She didn't think it was Luke who stole them, and she was pretty sure it wasn't Dr. Lyle. Miranda had denied it, and it didn't make a lot of sense for her to break into the machine to steal them if she was getting away with taking them one and two at a time, as it seemed she had been. It was possible she was working with Dr. Perez, who was prescribing far more of the powerful opioids than other physicians. But Miranda was the first person to enter the recovery room. Why hadn't any of the people who went into the room after her seen the machine open?

That left Olga. Olga, who had gone into the recovery room twice in the window that was in question, and who had been the last one in the room before Anne discovered the theft. Olga, who had a history of addiction. Anne hated to think that it could be her, not after she'd worked so hard to get and stay clean and get her son back, and found faith in the process. Just because someone had gotten clean didn't guarantee they would stay that way. Relapses happened far more than anyone hoped. And if Olga saw the medication being dispensed every day, but had no way to get at it herself... Well, it would be understandable, though no less tragic.

Anne hoped she was wrong. She wanted to see the footage again. Maybe there was some way to prove that it hadn't been Olga after all, and she'd just missed it. Anne pulled the thumb drive out of her purse, where she'd tucked it, and she inserted it into her laptop once again. She waited until the computer recognized it, and then she pressed start.

She played the footage back at double speed, slowing it down when she came to the spots where someone had gone into the room. Shirley and Paige moving the C-section patient out at 11:33. Miranda entering at 11:48 and exiting three minutes later. Olga going in at 11:55 and spending nearly eight minutes inside. Dr. Lyle at 12:06, emerging less than ninety seconds later. He'd just made a quick call. Luke Merritt at 12:24, emerging at 12:27. Olga going back again at 12:29, coming out less than a minute later. And then, just a moment later, Anne seeing the machine and stopping. There they all were. All the players right there on screen. But no further clues as to which of them had done it.

There had to be more. Someone had to have seen something. With all those people in the hallway, just a few feet from where someone had—quite violently—broken into the machine, how could no one have seen anything?

The police and the hospital had spoken to all the staff who'd been on the floor at that time. Had they talked to each of the patients too? Detective Lee had said they planned to. Had those interviews turned up anything? Anne looked back at the screen. There were so many potential witnesses. Surely one of them had some clue, had seen something that hadn't made sense at the time but would crystalize in retrospect. It was maddening that the security camera hadn't caught the thief in the act. But it was far from the only camera in the labor and delivery ward that day, Anne realized. Every single person on that floor had a phone, Anne was willing to wager.

All of them had cameras. And the maternity ward was a place where people were constantly taking videos and photos, capturing every moment of a child's new life. With all those cell phones on the ward, surely someone had a photo or a video or something that had captured some clue they had missed.

But how would she even start looking for those things? How could she find every single person—patients, as well as their friends and family—and ask if they had accidentally captured some crucial moment that would reveal the identity of the thief? Some image or video they didn't even realize contained a clue? They could probably track down the patients fairly easily, but could they start asking about their visitors? Even if they could, that would take so long, and they didn't have that kind of time.

Anne supposed it wasn't impossible. The hospital could put out a call for the public to help. Engage the media. They'd done it before. But in the wake of the bad publicity they'd already received, would they really go out and publicly ask for anyone who was there in the labor and delivery ward to search their phones to help them find the answer? That would be admitting they were stumped. Anne doubted Garrison would want to do that. She could ask him in the morning, but she was prepared to hear a no.

Anne stared at the screen, letting her eyes go blurry. And slowly, an idea began to form. What if they didn't need to talk to everyone who had walked up and down that hallway during the right time frame? What if they only needed to focus on the ones who reasonably could have seen something? Those would be the people who had walked past the recovery room while one of the suspects was in there, or going in or coming out. How many of those could there be?

When she'd viewed the footage before, she'd only focused on the suspects themselves entering. What if she paid attention instead to the other people in the videos, the ones she hadn't noticed before?

Anne backed the footage up and started playing it once again, and this time, she focused on the people who didn't enter the recovery room, the people who were just walking past at opportune times—

And she couldn't believe what she'd missed on her first viewing.

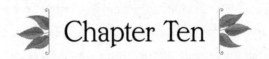

Chapter Ten

Thursday morning, Anne texted her friends before she left for the hospital. I have a potential lead. Can you meet me in the gift shop at 9?

I'll be there, Evelyn wrote.

Yep, Joy said.

I'll do my best, Shirley responded.

Anne checked in at the volunteer room and offered to start with delivering flowers, which gave her a perfect excuse to head down to the gift shop.

When Anne walked in, she found Joy in the back room, trimming the ends off a bunch of soft pink camellias and vibrant darker pink dahlias.

"Hello," Anne said. "Those are beautiful."

"Fresh from the garden," Joy said. "Hey, I wanted to ask you. I emailed Olga yesterday to check in."

"Just to check in?" Anne gave a knowing smile.

"Well, maybe not entirely," Joy said. "Anyway, she's not working today, but she invited me to come over to her place after work for coffee. Would you be interested in coming along?"

"Of course I would. But I would hate to impose."

"She specifically said you were invited too. She didn't come out and say it, but I suspect she wants to talk about what happened Monday."

"In that case, don't you dare go without me."

"If you can stick around a bit after your shift, we can head over together."

"Perfect."

"What's perfect?" They both looked up as Evelyn walked into the gift shop. Today she wore a peacock-blue button-down with an enamel peacock pin on her lapel.

"We're going to talk to Olga later to hopefully learn the truth about what she was doing in that room," Joy explained. "You're welcome to come too, but it's after my shift."

"Sadly, I've got a budget meeting then," Evelyn said. "But you two have fun."

"Have fun doing what?" Shirley had entered the gift shop, and Anne repeated the story.

"I wish I could make it, but I have to leave early to take my mom to the doctor."

"Is everything okay?" Joy had a soft spot for Shirley's mom, Regina. Actually, they all did. She was a wonderful person, and had a great sense of humor too. Regina had also left quite a legacy of excellence as a nurse at Mercy decades before.

"Just a normal checkup with her neurologist," Shirley said. Shirley lived with her mother because of Regina's memory issues. It was a lot to deal with on top of her work, but Shirley rarely complained. "So what do you have?"

Anne explained why she had decided to take another look at the footage, and Joy moved the flowers and cleared space at the table for her laptop. Anne inserted the thumb drive, pulled up the video, and started it from the beginning, again slowing it down when any one of the four suspects went in or out of the room. "Pay attention to the other people in the video," Anne said.

"Like her?" Evelyn pointed as, on screen, Miranda went into the recovery room. Evelyn indicated a woman in a bathrobe and slippers, hunched over, shuffling down the hallway, with a helpless-looking man following, his hand on her back.

"I don't see a camera," Anne said. "So I doubt she has footage for us."

"She didn't see anything," Shirley said. "She's deep in the throes of labor. She wouldn't notice much, even if it was right in front of her."

Anne had also suspected the same thing, so she let the video continue to play. While Miranda was in the recovery room, a few nurses went past.

"The police and hospital have already talked to all the nurses, so I'm not concerned with them," Anne said. "If they saw anything, the police already know about it."

The nurses continued off-screen, and no one was in the hallway when Miranda came out.

"There's Olga," Evelyn said when Olga pushed her cart into the room at 11:55. No one else was in the hallway at that moment. But in the eight minutes she was inside the room, half a dozen doctors and nurses went by. Once again, Anne wasn't bothered by them; they had already been interviewed. There was also an older man and a woman who walked by, a toddler between them, holding a bunch of balloons.

"Grandparents on their way to meet a new member of the family," Joy said. "I remember them. They bought those balloons here. The little girl was so excited to meet her new brother."

"This guy's got a camera," Anne said. The grandpa had a camera on a strap over his shoulder, but none of them had a phone or a camera out. "But he's not using it, so that's not helpful. But here. Take a look at her." She pointed at the screen as, seven minutes into Olga's time in the recovery room, a woman walked down the hallway holding a newborn baby in one arm, her phone on a selfie stick in the other. She was making a video of some kind and was glammed up with her hair curled and lipstick on.

"Wait. Did this woman really just give birth?" Joy asked, shaking her head. "And now she's that made up?"

"Why is she parading up the hallway making a video with her newborn baby posed like a prop?" Evelyn asked.

"I don't know how she's even walking," Anne said. After Anne's births, she hadn't wanted to move for days. "But she has a camera out at the right time. She might have captured something."

"I remember her," Shirley said. "She was some kind of YouTube star or something."

"A what?" Evelyn had one eyebrow raised.

"She makes a living posting videos of herself on the web. I was in her room for a bit, and she explained that she'd been sharing her pregnancy journey with her followers, and she was excited to show them a video introducing the new baby." Shirley looked as skeptical as Evelyn.

"Is that a thing you can make a living doing?" Joy asked.

"Apparently, you can make a lot of money doing it if you drum up enough followers." Shirley shrugged. "Anyway, that's what the deal is."

"What's her name?"

"I couldn't tell you her real name even if I wanted to," Shirley said. She referred to HIPAA privacy regulations. "But I can tell you that she posts her videos under the name Shameless Sarah."

"Shameless Sarah?" Anne repeated.

"Something about not letting other people make her feel bad about her life? I don't know. I just know what she told me."

"It shouldn't be that hard to find her," Anne said. "I can look her up."

"The video she was making has probably already been posted," Joy said. "See if you can find anything there on her YouTube channel."

"I will. For now, let's keep going."

She pressed play again, and the video kept rolling. Olga came out to an empty hallway, and shortly afterward, Dr. Lyle went into the room. "There." She paused the video.

Kitty, a nurse, pushed a rolling clear acrylic bassinet, the kind they used to transport an infant from the patient's room to the nursery. A tiny baby, wrapped up like a burrito, was being wheeled to the nursery, and the two were accompanied by a man—a new father, Anne was sure—holding up his phone. They passed by the recovery room while Dr. Lyle was inside.

"That guy is taking a video," Anne said.

"He's making a video of his kid being wheeled to the nursery?" Evelyn shook her head. "Who would ever want to watch that?"

"You'd be shocked at some of the stuff new parents take videos of," Shirley said. "The other day I came in while a dad was taking a video of his baby's first diaper change. And I've seen plenty of fathers getting a video of the birth itself."

"Why would anyone want to relive that?" Joy looked as horrified as Anne felt.

Shirley shrugged. "It's beautiful, really. The moment a new life enters the world? That's special, no question about it. But I don't know that I'd want a video of it happening to me, personally."

Anne shuddered just thinking about it.

"In any case, this guy probably just wanted to capture every moment," Shirley said.

"Which is convenient for us, because he appeared to have pointed his camera toward the recovery room," Joy said. "If we could get ahold of the video from his phone, we might be able to see inside the room."

"Maybe," Anne said. "But footage of what? Of Dr. Lyle talking to his wife about his sick son?"

"We should follow every lead," Evelyn said.

She was right. It was possible his phone had captured some useful clue in the video he was taking. Unlikely, but possible. "So how do we find him?"

"That's what I was hoping you guys could help me figure out."

"I have no clue who he is," Shirley said. "He wasn't in one of my rooms."

"Hang on." Joy pointed at something on his shirt. "What's that?"

"Is that a logo?" Anne squinted, trying to get a better look. The guy wore a dark-colored polo with something on the left breast. "Maybe it's one of those horse shirts?"

"No," Joy said, shaking her head. "Wilson had a lot of those, and that logo is much smaller than this."

"This almost looks like the logo for that grocery store chain," Evelyn said.

Anne knew which store she meant. And now that Evelyn had pointed it out, it did look remarkably like the two circles—one red, one green—that made up the logo of the local supermarket franchise.

"So maybe he works at the store," Shirley said.

"Either that or he's just an enthusiast," Anne said.

When none of her friends responded, Anne quickly added, "That was a joke. I'm sure he's employed there."

"He must have been on duty when he got the call that his wife was in labor," Evelyn said.

"But there have to be half a dozen of those stores in the area," Joy said. "Which one does he work for?"

"Hard to say. But I'm sure we can find out," Shirley said.

"The way his phone is pointed, he has an almost direct view into that recovery room," Evelyn said. "We've got to find him and check it out, even if we don't think Dr. Lyle really did it. We have to pursue every clue."

"I'll dig into it," Anne said. "Let's see what else there is." She started the video again, and the father and baby vanished off the screen, and Dr. Lyle came out a moment later. Anne let the video run and pointed out the only other person she'd identified as a potential lead, a grandfather who came out of the postpartum room directly across from the recovery room just before Luke Merritt left.

"He didn't have a phone or camera visible," Joy said.

"But it was nearly a direct line of sight from there to the recovery room," Evelyn said. "It's possible the grandfather saw something."

"I'm sure the police interviewed the patient," Joy said.

"But the patient wouldn't have seen anything if she was in the room on the bed. The grandpa would have been the one who saw Luke in the room," Anne said.

"I'll see if Garrison can tell us how to find him," Anne said, but she wasn't optimistic.

"But we have a couple of decent leads," Joy said. "The YouTuber and the grocery store guy both could have captured something in their videos."

It sounded so hopeless when she said it like that. But Anne wasn't going to give up hope. "I'll see if I can track either of them down today," Anne said.

Anne's first flower delivery was to the pediatric ward—one of Anne's least favorite places to go in the hospital. It was so sad to see children so sick, and Anne always went out of her way to try to cheer the kids up. Anne delivered the flowers to a little girl named Emily who was fighting leukemia, and she spent some time coloring with her at the small table in her room. Emily talked about how she missed her friends and her dog Waffles and couldn't wait to go home to play with her toys again.

Then Anne brought a bunch of flowers that included this morning's dahlias to a woman who had just had her hip replaced. After that, Anne returned to the maternity ward, bringing flowers to a mother trying to nurse newborn twins. Then Anne headed for the elevators to return downstairs, and she found Miranda waiting as well, looking down at her phone.

Anne felt awkward running into her after their encounter yesterday, but would it be more awkward if she didn't say anything and just pretended she didn't see her? Miranda would notice her at some point, if they were going to be sharing an elevator. It would be more weird if Miranda saw that Anne had seen her and didn't say anything. Anne decided she couldn't just ignore Miranda, no matter how much easier that might be, so she forced herself to put on her best Southern belle smile and step forward.

"Hi there, Miranda."

Miranda looked up and nodded. She wasn't upset to see Anne, necessarily. But she wasn't pleased, judging by the raised eyebrows.

"How's everything going?"

"It's fine." Miranda stepped forward and pushed the down button again, even though the light was already lit. "Busy day."

"It's funny how it comes in waves, isn't it?" Anne said. Her voice sounded too loud to her, too chipper, but Anne hoped Miranda couldn't tell.

There was an awkward silence for a moment. They both looked at the elevator doors, Anne willing them to open. But as the silence stretched out, Anne couldn't stand it. If being a pastor's wife had taught her anything, it was how to make conversation with anyone.

"This is some heat, isn't it?" she said. "I know it's always like this in the summer in Charleston, but I just can't help thinking it gets worse every year."

"It's the South," Miranda said with a shrug.

"At this time of year, I'm always dreaming about going somewhere else. I'm actually trying to plan a vacation right now, trying to figure out where we can go to get some relief."

Miranda nodded, a tense smile on her face. Her phone screen lit up, though it didn't ring audibly. Anne angled her neck. CRESTVIEW, the screen said. Anne didn't know what Crestview was, but maybe she should look into it, seeing as how often they were in contact with Miranda.

"I was doing some looking around at beach houses," Anne said. "But I don't know. I started checking into mountain cabins too. But my daughter wants to go to California, and my granddaughter wanted to go to Disney World, so I feel like I can't make everyone happy no matter what I pick."

Why was Anne telling this woman these things? She hadn't even really admitted the last part to herself. But the elevator doors remained closed, so Anne kept on talking.

"My daughter was deployed for some time, so I really want to make it special this year, you know? There are no guarantees when we'll be able to do it again. So I want everything to be perfect, and I guess that's making it really hard to make a decision. I think I'm getting myself all tied up in knots."

Miranda was looking at her now, but she wasn't saying anything.

"How about you?" Anne needed to quit talking. "Are you going on vacation this summer?"

"No," Miranda said with a pinched smile. "It's hard to get away, with my dad."

Just then, the elevator doors opened, and Miranda immediately stepped inside. Anne followed just behind, but the elevator was crowded, and Miranda had made her way to the back. Anne couldn't get close enough to her to follow up with questions about what she meant, and she wasn't about to start shouting questions from the front of the crowded space. It stopped again on the second floor, and then, finally, the doors opened into the lobby and they all began to exit. Miranda went immediately to the hallway that led to the Grove. It was clear she didn't want to continue her conversation with Anne.

Anne made a few more deliveries, and then she covered for Peggy at the front desk again, and while Peggy was eating her lunch, Anne spent some time watching videos from Shameless Sarah on the web. It wasn't hard to find her YouTube channel, and her most recent video was captioned THE MOST AMAZING MIRACLE—MEETING PENELOPE. Anne assumed Penelope must be the name of the baby. The video was just over five minutes long, and it was a compilation of clips. Anne watched Sarah and her husband getting ready to leave for the hospital, Sarah's heavy breathing in the passenger seat as her husband sped down the street, some shots of her grimacing in pain, even clips of her lying in the hospital bed, her legs up, pushing. Everything was covered, but Anne still couldn't believe anyone would want to put such personal images online. Those clips were followed by shots of Sarah reaching out to hold her baby for the first time, and then cradling a newborn that had been cleaned up and wrapped. Finally, in the last thirty seconds of the video was the footage Anne was looking for. She saw Sarah walking around the ward with a selfie stick and her newborn, talking about what an ordeal it was, not how it had all been worth it. Anne kept her eyes on the background of the video, knowing that Miranda Martel was inside the recovery room that was just to Sarah's right, but she didn't see anything or anyone coming in or out.

Based on what she saw here, it didn't seem likely that Shameless Sarah's video footage would shed much light on what had happened inside the recovery room, but Anne was still not going to give up. Instead, she clicked on the CONTACT button on the page, and she was given a whole list of email addresses she could use to contact Sarah. *Let's see.* Would it be management, booking, brand partnerships, film and video, or literary? Anne decided to just go with management, and she fired off an email explaining who she was and what she was looking for. There was no telling if anyone would read it or respond, but she hoped she would hear back.

Anne planned to do some research into the locations of the supermarket chain the guy in the other video worked for, but she didn't have a chance before Peggy returned from her break and Anne went off to help with discharge. She did get a text from Evelyn, though, asking her to come to Records when she had a minute, so when Anne was finally done with her shift at two, she walked back to Evelyn's office.

"She responded," Evelyn said.

"Who did?"

"Linda Michaelson. The great-granddaughter of Joshua Palmer."
Evelyn gestured for Anne to come around her desk and look at the
computer screen.

"Oh wow." Anne leaned closer to read the open email.

Evelyn,

    *Thank you for reaching out. I am surprised and delighted
to hear about the letters you found from my great-grandfather
Joshua Palmer. I am something of a self-appointed family historian, and I can tell you that his unknown fate was the source
of great consternation and sadness for his family. I know that
my grandfather, Joshua's son Aaron, spoke often in his later
years about how haunting it had been to grow up not knowing
what happened to his father. Aaron's mother, my great-
grandmother, never remarried, not knowing whether her husband was dead or alive. Though she would have mourned to
know the truth, she could have built a new life and had more
children with the certainty that Joshua was never coming
back, and I believe a second family would have been a great
comfort to her in her later years. Her diaries reveal a woman
deeply saddened and confused, but ever hopeful that her
beloved husband would someday return. I wish that she had
known that he would not.*

    *Your note said that he died of an infection, as so many
did, and that even in terrible pain he spoke lovingly of his
wife and child. It brings me no end of comfort to hear that.
Pain like that—with no relief and no possibility of drugs to*

bring comfort—changes people. I spent my career as a nurse on an oncology ward, and I know for a fact that the worst kind of pain shows your true colors. I am proud to know that my ancestor was thinking of his family to the very end.

I would love to see the letters you found. They would fill a hole in our family history. My daughter Annabelle lives in Columbia, and she is willing to pop over to Charleston to retrieve them if it can be arranged.

Yours,

Linda Michaelson

"Wow," Anne said. "I'm impressed that you located her at all, let alone found someone who knows the story."

"Families hold their stories close," Evelyn said. "Most of them do, anyway. Don't you know stories about your great-grandparents, even if you never knew them?"

Anne supposed she did. She'd heard many times of how her great-grandmother had wanted to go to college but hadn't been allowed to, and how she'd fallen head over heels for the naval officer in his dress uniform; how she'd hated it when he'd served overseas, afraid for him every moment.

"Are you going to arrange to get the letters to her daughter?"

"Absolutely. I'm going to email her right now."

"Let me know what happens."

Then Anne went to the gift shop to find Joy, and they walked out to the parking garage together and climbed into Joy's car. Joy punched Olga's address into her GPS, and then she blasted the air conditioning. Anne reveled in the cool air as they drove through the cobblestone streets of the historic downtown and out toward the highway. According to the map on the screen, Olga lived pretty far north, out by the airport.

As they drove, Anne recounted her awkward encounter with Miranda by the elevator. Joy laughed as she told her how uncomfortable it was.

"It was so awkward, after our conversation yesterday, where I basically accused her of stealing drugs from the hospital."

"If it's any consolation, it sounds like she didn't want to see you again just as much as you didn't want to see her."

"It went on forever, and all I knew to do was keep talking, so I just kept babbling."

"Oh man." Joy shook her head. "Those elevators are so slow too. It must have been painful, waiting for them to show up eventually."

"The thing is, our conversation out in the Grove didn't feel that awkward yesterday, so I didn't expect it to be as uncomfortable as it was. Yesterday, she was open and earnest, if direct. But today, as soon as I saw her, I wanted to turn and run the other way."

"No one wants to be suspected of theft," Joy said. "And that's what you were doing yesterday, right? Trying to find out if she was the one who stole the drugs? I can see why she'd be a little put off."

"Well, I hope we can get past it, because I'm probably going to run into her from time to time at the hospital."

"Do you think she did it?" Joy asked.

Anne waited a beat before she answered. "I don't know," she finally said. "I think it's very likely she's taken pills from the machines on a somewhat regular basis. There's enough evidence to suggest that. But I'm not sure it makes sense for her to be the one who broke into the machine on Monday."

"Why not?"

"For all the reasons we've discussed. Because she was the first one in the room, and surely one of the people who came in later would have seen the machine open. Because why would she change her tactic if skimming pills was working? Because, I don't know. I believed her when she said she didn't do it. Is that crazy?"

"Only if you're wrong." Joy tapped her fingers on the steering wheel. Anne played through the encounters with Miranda in her mind, trying to see if there was anything she was missing. As she thought back through the conversations, something niggled at the back of her mind.

"Do you know what Crestview is?" Anne asked.

"No idea." Joy flipped on her blinker and changed lanes on the highway. "What is it?"

"I don't know. I was hoping you would."

Joy laughed. "Maybe Siri can help."

Anne held up her phone and pressed the button on the side and said, "Hey Siri, what is Crestview?"

"Here are some Crestviews in your area," the phone replied in a woman's voice. Several links to websites popped up on the screen. Anne tapped the first one.

"There's a golf course over in Mt. Pleasant. And here's a nursing home."

"Do either of those sound right?"

"Huh." Anne thought for a minute. "You know, maybe. Miranda said they weren't going on vacation this year because it was hard with her dad. And I saw pictures of her with a man in a wheelchair on her social media."

"You think her father could be in the nursing home?" Joy asked.

"It's possible," Anne said. "Both times I was talking to her, they called, so if we're right, I hope everything is okay."

"Yikes." Joy gritted her teeth. "That's so hard."

"Hard enough that you might need a few pills to help you relax at the end of the day."

They both rode in silence, each lost in their own thoughts, until they pulled up in front of Olga's apartment building a few minutes later. It was a three-story wood-sided building, one of probably a dozen in the complex, and after they parked, they walked up the steps and down the hallway to the door marked 2R. Anne knocked, and Olga pulled it open. Her curly brown hair was escaping the ponytail she'd pulled it into, and she wore knee-length khaki shorts and an oversized T-shirt with Crocs. Anne realized she'd never seen her outside of her work uniform, but of course she wasn't wearing that at home.

"Come in." Olga stepped aside and ushered them into the living room. The beige carpet was stained in spots, and the faded black couch was accompanied by two mismatched armchairs. Bins along the far wall held soccer cleats and shin guards and basketballs, and a large gold cross was the sole decoration on the walls. "Please, have a seat." She gestured for them to sit on the couch. "Would you like some coffee?" Her voice, with its vague Eastern European accent had a lilting, musical quality to it.

Anne didn't usually drink caffeine this late in the day, but she thought it might be rude to refuse. "That sounds great." She sat down on the couch and sank deep in the cushion.

"Yes, please," Joy echoed.

"One moment." The kitchen was tucked in behind the dining nook at the far end of the room. Olga poured three cups of coffee into thick ceramic mugs, and she brought them over and set them on the low coffee table in front of the couch. She went back to the kitchen and retrieved a bowl of sugar and a pitcher of milk, and after she set them all down, she held up one finger, walked down the hallway, and knocked on a door. Anne heard some mumbling, and then she heard Olga say something in a language Anne didn't understand. Her son must be in his room. She picked up one of the mugs of coffee, added some milk and sugar, took a sip, and tried not to gag.

"She makes her coffee strong," Joy said, preemptively reaching for the sugar. "We had to ask her to tone it down when she was prepping the carafe for the church coffee hour."

Anne nodded and added another spoonful of sugar and a good pour of milk.

A moment later, Olga came back out and took a seat in a striped armchair.

"Thank you for coming to talk to me," she said and then took a deep breath. "First of all, Anne, I am sorry I lied to you. I told you I wasn't in the recovery room, and that wasn't true. I didn't want to tell you the truth, because I was afraid, but my sponsor has since reminded me that people finding out about my past was better than getting fired."

"Thank you," Anne said. "I knew what you'd told me wasn't true—we saw the security camera footage that showed you'd been in that room not once but twice. But I was curious about why you said that."

Olga picked up one of the mugs of coffee and took a sip. She looked down at the coffee for a moment, as if trying to steel herself.

"I was afraid," she said. "I knew people would suspect me, both because I had been in the room where the machine was, and because, well, because of my past. I don't know—" She let out a breath. "Did Joy tell you?"

"Joy told me that you worked very hard to overcome addiction," Anne said.

Olga nodded. "I don't know that you ever overcome it. But by God's grace, I got clean, and I have been clean for nearly two years. I haven't touched a pill since, not even Tylenol."

"That's very impressive," Anne said.

"It's a daily struggle, even now. But I fight the temptation, for Alex's sake."

"That's your son?"

She nodded. "When I lost him, when he was taken into protective custody, that's when I knew I had to make a change. I'd thought I was holding it together before then, that maybe no one knew how much I was struggling, but then he mentioned something to his teacher about my pills...and then Child Protective Services came and took him away."

"That must have been so hard," Joy said.

"It was terrible. But it was the best thing that ever happened. Sometimes I think God allows us to lose all ability to do anything but turn to Him, you know?"

"And He is always there, ready to help if we do," Joy said.

Olga continued. "That was me hitting bottom, watching them take Alex and give him to another family to raise. That was when I got serious about the meetings at the church, and it was at the church where I...well, where everything changed." She took another sip. Anne was still working up the courage to try her doctored coffee again. How was Olga drinking it straight? "Where I grew up, in Bulgaria...we did not have churches and things like this. It's different now, but when I was growing up, it was illegal to go to church."

Anne had a vague notion that Bulgaria was a Communist country, or had been, but she felt silly asking. Was it one of the countries that had been behind the Iron Curtain? Shouldn't she know things like this?

"So I had never had any real exposure to church as a kid, and when I came here, I just thought... I don't know what I thought. That people who went there were weirdos. That they were weak, dependent on some stories that could not possibly be true. But then, when I started attending meetings at the church, I started hearing stories about Jesus."

"They talked about those at the NA meetings?" Anne asked.

"No, not at the meetings themselves. It was all about a Higher Power there. But we were often in the building when different groups and Bible studies were being held. Sometimes, I would sit outside the youth room when the youth minister was preaching, and I would listen to the stories he told. It seemed incredible—that this Man died to save everyone. That He died to save me. It was preposterous. But I couldn't stop listening."

Anne never tired of hearing stories of how people first came to faith. Every single one of them was special to the Lord, and such a powerful testimony of His love.

"One night, when I was sitting outside the youth room, it just hit me different, you know? I couldn't explain it, but it was like…have you ever heard the term 'thin places'?"

"A place where the veil between this world and the eternal world is thin," Anne said.

Olga nodded. "For whatever reason, sitting in that hallway listening to a pastor try to get through to a group of rowdy teenagers, I felt it. It was like I was touching heaven somehow. I don't know how to explain it, but it felt like God was there with me. You know?"

"I do," Anne said, doing her best to hold back tears.

"I knew it was true. This impossible thing, this incredible story—it was more true, and more real, than anything else in this world."

"Praise God," Joy said quietly.

"It wasn't like everything in my life got better after that," Olga said. "Far from it. But I had a power I hadn't had before, and I fought hard. The Holy Spirit, I now know. I was finally able to get clean, and I got a job at the hospital. It was not glamorous, but it was steady, and after many months, I got Alex back." Anne wondered where Alex's father was in all this, but she didn't ask. It was even more impressive that Olga had done all this on her own.

"What made you want to work at the hospital?" Anne asked. "If you were fighting so hard to get clean?"

"Maybe this sounds silly, but it never even occurred to me that I would be anywhere near pills. I was just the housekeeper, you know?

I emptied trash cans, stripped beds. I did not even realize what was in those machines for many months. They weren't part of my job, so I didn't pay attention to them. And by the time I figured it out, I had Alex back. Even if I could have gotten into the machines, I wouldn't have."

"Do you know how to work them now?" Anne asked. She had spent enough time in the hospital that she might know where to find each medication.

"I know you need a nurse's ID and also a matching fingerprint," Olga said. "I wouldn't know what to do once I got into the system from there."

"Do you know where the C-section kits are kept?" Anne asked.

"I don't even know what a C-section kit is," Olga said. "Is that what was in the trash?"

"One element from the kit was found in the trash," Joy said. "I believe you were the one who found it?"

"That's right." Olga nodded. "It was when I was emptying the trash can later that afternoon. I wasn't able to go back into the room for some time, because the police had taped it off. But after they left, I was finally able to go in and clean it up. There was black dust on all the surfaces, and I didn't even know at first that that meant they were dusting for fingerprints. There was so much trash in the bin, and the floor was filthy. So many people walking back and forth all day. When I went to empty the trash, I felt something heavy in it. Usually it's just plastic wrappers, paper gowns, gloves, papers, that kind of thing. But this was a piece of metal of some kind. I fished it out and showed it to Cliff Fox."

Anne recognized the name of the head of Maintenance.

"He told me he was going to turn it in, just in case," Olga continued. "It wasn't until later in the week I was told it was used to pry the machine open. Then I was glad I had been wearing gloves while I cleaned. I already knew they suspected me. Cliff knew about my history, so I figured others did too. And several people had already questioned me about that day, including you." She glanced at Anne. "I had nothing to do with it, but I knew people thought I did."

"So what were you doing in the recovery room Monday?" Anne asked. "If you had nothing to do with the break-in?"

Olga set her coffee down on the table and took a deep breath. "Alex has been having trouble in school. I know it's been—it's been very hard for him. I gather the foster family he was with for all those months didn't treat him well. And of course, I wasn't exactly the best parent before that either, not while I was using. So it's no surprise. But on Monday, I got a call from the principal asking me to come pick him up. He was being suspended again. Fighting. Again."

"Oh dear." Anne started to see where this was going.

"We're not allowed to use our phones on the floor. Not where patients can see us. So I ducked into the room when I saw it was the school calling."

That was three of the suspects who claimed to have gone into the room to use their phones. Could they all be telling the truth?

"You were in the recovery room for some time," Joy said. "Nearly eight minutes."

"I was begging the principal to give him one more chance. The last two times he was in a fight, it was because the other boys had been teasing him, and both hit him first. From what I gathered, it was the same situation in this case."

"Did you convince the principal?" Anne asked.

"He told me we would discuss it when I came to the school. I told him I couldn't, I was on duty. They expected me to just leave, but I don't have the kind of job where I can do that. I tried to get a friend to help, but I couldn't get ahold of her. They made Alex stay in the principal's office until I could go pick him up. It was nearly five by that point. But in the end, yes, he is giving Alex another try."

Anne's heart grieved for Olga. It would be so hard for any mother to hear that her son was being bullied. Poor Alex.

"Did you notice if the Pyxis machine had been broken into at the time you were in the room?" Joy asked.

"I honestly do not know. I was not looking at it, or at anything really. I was only thinking about what would happen if Alex was kicked out of school, and how wrong it is that they do not stop the other kids from making fun of him." She sighed. "It could have been smashed to pieces, I don't know."

"What about when you went back into the room the second time?" Anne asked. "Why was that?"

"My friend was calling me back but only to say that she was helping her mother and couldn't get to the school."

"And did you notice the machine at that point?" Anne asked.

"I wish I could tell you I had seen it. That would make me seem less guilty, I know. But the truth is, I didn't. I guess it must have been open at that point, since I gather that it was very shortly after that that you discovered it, Anne." She shrugged. "But I can only tell the truth, and that is that I was so distracted that I didn't notice."

Anne believed her. She didn't want to—she was running out of suspects, and Olga had seemed like such a strong contender—but she did. Which left Anne with a dilemma. All four of the suspects who had gone into that recovery room during the window of the theft denied it, and they all seemed to be telling the truth. She believed every one of them. But clearly, one of them was lying. Someone had to be.

The only problem was, Anne had no clue which one it was.

Before they headed back to the hospital, Joy suggested they stop by the local branch of the grocery store chain to see if they could find the man who had taken the cell phone video of the newborn being wheeled down the hallway. Joy was going out to dinner with Roger Gaylord tonight—a wealthy benefactor for the hospital and someone Joy had been seeing more often lately—but she had some time. Anne had to pick up Addie at camp again, but not for another hour, so they programmed the address into the GPS and started driving.

"Are you excited about your vacation?" Joy asked as she maneuvered into the left lane.

"I don't know," Anne said. "I mean, yes, I will be, if I ever figure out where we're going."

"You still haven't decided?"

Anne had talked to Joy about it last week, and Anne had been stressed about it back then.

"I think I'm paralyzed by indecision," Anne said.

"And that pesky perfectionism," Joy said.

"What do you mean? I'm not a perfectionist."

Joy only raised an eyebrow in response.

"What? I'm not."

"It's understandable, in this case," Joy said. "You don't know when it's going to happen again. You want to make it special. I just hope you don't put so much pressure on yourself to make it awesome that you end up not having fun."

"It will be fun," Anne said. "I'll make sure it is."

"That's the spirit. You'll all have fun, even if you have to force them into it."

Anne sighed. "I just want to make everyone happy, and I don't know how to do that. They've each suggested something completely different."

"I don't know that it's your job to make everyone happy," Joy said. "Vacations aren't necessarily about each person getting what they want. They're about stepping away from the ordinary and being together with people you love, hopefully getting some rest and doing some fun things while you're at it."

"I mean, I guess you're right, in a way," Anne said. "I don't know." She wasn't sure she wanted to talk about this with Joy. Anne loved Joy dearly, but Joy didn't necessarily have the same concerns as Anne. For one thing, budget had never been an issue for Joy. Her husband, Wilson, had worked in the oil industry, and they had taken lavish vacations all over the world through the years. Joy never flaunted her money, but it was clear she was comfortably well-off. Anne guessed Joy had never had to price out budget motels to see if she could afford a cross-country road trip. "Where would you go, if you were me?"

"Italy," Joy said without hesitation. "You've never seen Rome, and you must."

Anne would love to walk down those ancient streets, see the Sistine Chapel and the Trevi Fountain, and eat pizza and pasta and gelato until she couldn't fit into her pants.... It sounded heavenly.

"Okay, but realistically?" Anne said. "Assuming European vacations are not in the realm of possibility?"

"I'd do something really simple," Joy said. "A tent in the woods or a rustic cabin of some kind. Somewhere where you could be together with the people you love with the fewest number of distractions."

It did sound nice, Anne had to admit. But still. Joy made it seem so simple, and it was anything but. She'd looked into cabins. You still had to find one, and all the good ones were booked up. She decided to try to change the subject. "How about you? You have a vacation coming up, right? Where are you going?"

"Nowhere fancy," Joy said. "Just back to Texas to visit family. Sabrina and the girls are coming too. We're going to see people we haven't seen in a while and catch up."

"Not Rome? Or Paris?" Anne was teasing, and Joy seemed to understand that.

"For one thing, Texas is every bit as amazing as Paris and Rome, thank you very much," Joy said, laughing. "Maybe you've never seen that wide-open prairie sky, but it's like nowhere else in the world. And besides, as amazing as those places are—and they are amazing, don't get me wrong—they've got nothing on the pleasures of simply being with people you love."

Anne contemplated Joy's words as they pulled into the parking lot for the grocery store and made their way down the crowded aisles to find a place to park. They parked, walked through the lot, and stepped into the store and looked around. To the left was the produce aisle, with a display of sweet peaches and mangoes next to plastic containers of strawberries, blueberries, and raspberries. To the right were the checkouts, with the deli and bakery beyond. All the employees wore the same royal blue polo with the store's logo on the breast.

"This place is huge," Joy said, and Anne nodded. Along the front wall was a coffee bar, a bank kiosk, and bottle recycling, and beyond it—ah. There was a door marked MANAGER.

"Let's try that," Anne said. Joy followed her, and they knocked.

"Come in." The voice was muffled by the closed door, but it was clear enough. Anne pushed open the door, and they stepped into the small, windowless office. The walls were beige, and the floor was beige, and the man behind the desk wore a blue shirt over beige pants.

"Oh, I thought you were Dwayne," he said, looking up at them behind thick glasses.

"Sorry, we're not Dwayne," Anne said. She had no idea who Dwayne was. "Are you the manager?"

"That's right." He stood and reached out his hand. "Manuel Reyes. How can I help you?"

"We're trying to find an employee who had a baby Monday morning," Anne said. "Or perhaps Sunday night."

"No one here was recently pregnant," Manuel said.

"It was a man," Joy clarified.

Manuel narrowed his eyes and tilted his head.

"So, technically, I guess he didn't have the baby," Joy said. "But his wife or partner or girlfriend did."

"Huh." Manuel leaned back in his chair and looked up. "Why?"

"We're from the hospital," Anne said. "Trying to follow up about a hospital matter."

It was weak, and Anne knew it. But he didn't call her on it like she'd thought he might.

"Jeremy over in the deli had a grandchild last week," he said. "Could he be who you mean?"

"No, I don't think so," Joy said. "We're looking for a younger man."

"Well, I don't know everything about the personal lives of all my employees," Manuel said. "But I kind of think of this like a family, and I don't think anyone here just became a parent. Hey, Lindsay!"

Anne realized he had shouted this last part at the checker at the closest check-out lane. She turned. She had dark lipstick, and her long hair was dyed a deep black. "Yeah, boss?"

"Do you know of anyone here who just became a father?"

"No." She shook her head. "There's no one here who just had a baby."

Manuel turned back to Anne and Joy. "You're sure the person you're looking for works here?"

"We know he worked at a branch of this grocery store," Joy said. "But we're not sure of the location."

"Ah. In that case, maybe you should try one of the other locations."

"Thanks so much," Anne said.

"We appreciate it."

There were only five more locations to check. The guy they were looking for had to work at one of them.

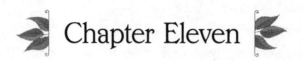

Chapter Eleven

ANNE AND JOY STOPPED OFF at one more location of the grocery store chain on the way back to the hospital, but they didn't find the man with the phone taking a video of his new baby. Joy dropped Anne off at her car, and then Anne drove home through rush hour traffic. She made it just in time for Addie's pickup, and they spent the next few hours eating dinner and playing a card game called Exploding Kittens. It was a silly game, and it felt good to laugh and get her mind off everything going on and just enjoy time with Addie. But as they were cleaning up, Anne's phone rang. Nick.

"Why don't you go in there with your grandfather for a while?" Anne suggested, nodding her head toward the living room.

"But he's watching baseball." Addie wrinkled her nose.

"Just for a little bit. I have to talk to this person."

"This person" being Addie's great-uncle Nick, whom she'd only met once, when she was a baby. Addie scooted off toward the living room, and Anne took a deep breath before she answered the call.

"Hello?"

"Hi, Anne. How are things?" He sounded good. He sounded like Nick. Anne felt her shoulders relax a bit as she realized he was clean, for now anyway.

"I'm okay. How are you?"

"I'm fine. Everything is all right here. I'm sorry it took me a bit to call you back."

"That's all right. I did worry when I didn't hear from you, though. You're...doing okay?"

"Yes. I'm still going to my meetings, if that's what you mean. I talk to my sponsor every day. I haven't taken anything in eighteen months."

"That's wonderful. I'm so glad to hear it."

"I was just busy finishing a table I was working on for a client. I've gotten a lot of referrals recently, which is nice."

Nick had taken up woodworking in recent years, and Anne was glad to hear it was keeping him busy.

"That's great. And your job is going well?"

"Yes, it is. I'm still at the factory. It's not exactly my dream job, but it's steady, and I'm working hard to find something else now that things have...stabilized. I'm seeing the kids again too. It's been great to be able to visit with them."

"I'm glad to hear it," Anne said.

"What's up? Is there any reason you're so interested all of a sudden?"

Ouch. That hurt. "I'm interested because I care about you. You're my brother." But it was true that she didn't call him all that often. "And because something happened at work, and it made me think of you."

"What was it?"

"There was a theft."

"And a theft brought me to mind?" He was teasing, that was clear by his tone. "Anne, I'm an addict, not a burglar." He was trying to make light of his disease, and Anne wasn't sure if that was a good sign or not.

"Someone stole a large amount of medication."

"Ah, I see. What did they steal? And how?"

"They broke into a Pyxis machine—that's a machine that dispenses medication—"

"Wait, like a vending machine but for drugs?"

"Kind of like that. And they stole opioids. Lots of them. Let's see. I believe it was Demerol, oxycodone, hydromorphone, and I think one other. Fentanyl, maybe?"

He let out a low whistle. "Someone wasn't messing around."

"From what I understand, they're very powerful drugs."

"And highly controlled, in most cases. They don't know who did it?"

"We have a list of suspects, but we aren't sure which one it was."

"We? Are you investigating this?"

"Unofficially," Anne said. "I'm just helping if I can. Obviously the police are actually the ones doing most of the investigating."

"Huh."

"What?"

"It's just an interesting mix, is all. Obviously someone knew what they were doing, going for those pills specifically."

"Because they're so powerful?"

"And so valuable. A haul like that? Assuming he took more than a few of each, that would be worth a lot on the streets."

Anne hated that he knew that.

"It's also an interesting mix. Most people who were dependent on a drug—they would probably just go for that one in particular. Whoever cleaned this machine out wasn't very picky, it seems. I mean, they appear to have known what they wanted, but they just took all the drugs. It wasn't someone with an addiction to a particular one. Or, I mean, maybe it was, it's hard to say."

"What are you getting at?" Anne asked.

"Just that the mix makes me think it's more likely that someone was getting what they could for other people, rather than for themselves, if you know what I mean."

"To sell."

"Probably. Or someone is in a lot of pain, and they just want anything that will help." He was quiet for a minute and then sighed. "Then again, that fentanyl is interesting."

"How so?"

"That stuff is really powerful. It's one of the most powerful out there—like, fifty to a hundred times more powerful than morphine."

"Yikes."

"Most of the stuff available on the streets isn't medical-grade but made in labs and not as good."

"Like, meth labs?"

"Sort of." He was quiet for a moment. "On the streets, it's often cut with other things. It's also really easy to overdose because it's so strong. Something like 50 percent of overdoses involve fentanyl in some form."

Anne wondered, but didn't ask, if he knew that from personal experience. She wasn't sure she'd ever had a conversation in which Nick was so honest and open about the drugs he'd been exposed to, and no doubt taken. Anne read it as a sign that he was truly on the path to becoming healthy again.

"There's a guy in one of my groups who was addicted to fentanyl. He was an anesthesiologist, if you can believe it. I thought it was kind of crazy, but apparently that's more common than you'd think. The job is super-stressful, and they have access to everything, all the best stuff, and before they know it they're in too deep. He said they even had to go through training on how to avoid addiction in medical school, and still it happened to him. It's apparently fairly common."

"Huh."

"What?"

"One of our suspects is an anesthesiologist. But I don't think it was him."

"It may not be. The fentanyl just reminded me of my friend, that's all. My money is still on someone looking to sell it. Do any of your suspects have a way to unload a lot of drugs quickly?"

"Yes," Anne thought of Luke. "But I don't think it's him either."

Nick laughed. "Who do you think it is, then?"

"I wish I knew."

"Well, if I know you, you'll figure it out soon," Nick said. "I just hope it's not too late."

"Not too late for what?" But even as she said it, Anne realized that she knew.

"Take care of yourself," Nick said instead of answering her question.

"You too."

"Love you, sis."

"I love you too."

Anne set down the phone, unsettled. She was glad to hear from Nick, and it genuinely sounded like he was doing well. Working hard to get his life back on track. But still, she worried. He'd been doing well before too.

She thought about what he'd said about fentanyl while she said goodbye to Addie and chatted with Lili.

"You're coming over for dinner tomorrow, right?" Anne asked. That had become the routine for most Fridays this summer.

"We'll be here," Lili said.

When they were gone, Ralph let her know that Sal wanted him to bring his car into the shop in the morning. "Would you be able to drive over there with me and take me to the hospital after that?"

"Of course. And I'll bring you home after work."

"Well, I'm glad of that," Ralph said, laughing. "I must be doing something right if my wife will still bring me home at the end of the day." He sat down on the edge of the bed. "I have to work this Saturday too. Joey has the day off. Hopefully I'll have the car back by then, but if not…"

"I'm happy to be your chauffeur," Anne said.

"I'm glad to hear it." He grinned at her. "How did your call with Nick go?"

Anne told Ralph about their chat, and then she asked, "What do you know about Brendan Lyle?"

"I know he makes a great barbeque and is better at golf than I'll ever be. His mother brags about him constantly, and his father was a thorn in my side for years. Never wanted to spend a penny of the church's endowment, even on necessary repairs. I also know that the cost of Brendan's wedding could have fed a small country for a year. Why?" Ralph set his toothbrush down and rinsed his mouth.

"I'm just thinking." Anne watched Ralph in the mirror as she rubbed lotion into her hands. Ralph never betrayed the confidence of the people he counseled. That was what made him such a trust-worthy pastor. Would he tell her anything, even if he knew?

"About what?"

"Do you know if he's ever had any problem with substance abuse?"

"Oh. I see." He used the back of his sleeve to wipe his mouth. "You know I couldn't tell you anything I learned in counseling, even if I did know something."

"You're right. I know." She smoothed the lotion into her cuticles. "I'm sorry for asking." Sometimes she hated that Ralph was such a good man.

"Why are you asking?"

"Brendan is one of the people who might have broken into the Pyxis machine at the hospital," Anne said. "And I didn't really con-sider him seriously until Nick said something about another anes-thesiologist he knows from one of his groups. He said it's not that uncommon for anesthesiologists to become addicted to opioids."

Ralph's only answer was to lean in and press a kiss on her fore-head, and then he turned for bed.

Chapter Twelve

FRIDAY MORNING, ANNE WOKE UP with a start. Something Nick had said the night before had crystalized in her mind while she slept, and when she put it together with a few other clues, she had a thought she wanted to check out. Anne climbed out of bed, Ralph still snoring beside her, and crept into the kitchen to start the coffee.

She lifted the lid on her laptop and opened her email. There was no response from Shameless Sarah's management. Then she went back to Miranda Martel's Facebook page. She scrolled through it until she came to the photo of the man in a wheelchair. This time, Anne looked at the background. He was in some kind of managed care facility, that was clear from the cinderblock walls and the scrubs worn by the nurse standing next to him in the photo. The group was posed outside the door to his room, judging by the nameplate that said RICK MARTEL on it. Anne was willing to bet it was Crestview, though she didn't see anything in the photo that proved that. She began to scroll back through Miranda's posts and found one from a few months previously where Miranda was asking for prayer for her dad, who was in a lot of pain as his cancer advanced.

Goodness. Anne hated to read that he had cancer and that he was in pain. How awful. She scrolled through a few months before that and saw a series of posts asking people to pray for her father's surgery. He had pancreatic cancer, she read, and had had part of his pancreas surgically removed back in February. Miranda had asked for prayers before, during, and after the surgery and then shared a post giving thanks that the doctors were hopeful. But Anne was reading backward, so she knew that while the surgery might have been successful, the cancer was advancing and he was in a lot of pain.

Yikes. Anne felt terrible for him, and for Miranda. Watching someone you love suffer like that—it was beyond comprehension. When Ariane had been fighting leukemia, she'd been in so much pain, and Anne would have done anything in the world to take it away from her. Anything she could have to make her daughter feel better. Anne guessed Miranda felt the same about her father. But how far would she be willing to go to ease his pain? Was there any chance...?

The coffee maker spurted and hissed, and Anne got up to pour herself a cup. She heard Ralph stirring in the bedroom. It was still early, but...she checked the website for the grocery store chain and looked at the locations in the area. They all opened at seven, which meant someone should be there to talk to her. It took three tries, but she finally found the right location of the grocery store chain.

"I'm hoping to speak with an employee who had a baby born at Mercy Hospital either Sunday or Monday," Anne explained to the manager. She was already used to having to explain that she wasn't looking for a pregnant woman but a new father, and for the confusion the managers always showed, but this time, the manager said, "Oh, you mean Colton?"

"That might be right," Anne said, scribbling down the name on the back of an electric bill. "What's his last name?"

"Brown. Colton Brown. He works in the stockroom. He ran out of here right in the middle of his shift Sunday when he got the call that his girlfriend was in labor. I don't know where she had the baby, but he's the only one at this location who fits the bill."

"That sounds like he's probably the right guy," Anne said. "Would you be able to help me contact him?"

"I don't know if I can do that," the manager said. "What did you say you needed to talk to him for?"

"I was hoping to discuss an incident that happened at the hospital Monday," Anne said. "He's not under any kind of suspicion," she added quickly. "I'm just hoping he may have seen something."

"He's a good kid. Always on time for his shifts, does a good job. Never given me any kind of trouble. He's too young to be a dad, in my opinion, but he'll do his best."

"Do you have any idea where I might be able to find contact information for him?" Anne asked.

"I'm afraid not," the manager said.

"Thank you. I understand," Anne said, and then she hung up. She pulled up a search window on her phone and typed in the name Colton Brown. She sorted through several pages of results, but she found him—his Instagram page had photos of him snuggling a newborn, with the caption *Love at first sight. Amberlynn did amazing and Brady is home and doing well. Thanks for all your prayers.* You couldn't see the baby's face, just a burrito of blankets, but in the photo, Colton studied his newborn, and his gaze held so much love.

It was the guy in the security camera footage, the guy who had taken the video that may have shown what was happening inside the recovery room at the time of the theft. Now all she had to do was find him. He lived in West Ashley, according to his bio. He was too young to have his address listed in the phone book, she was pretty sure. Only people with landlines were there, and Anne didn't know anyone this young who had a landline. She tried googling his name and WEST ASHLEY, SC and found an online petition he'd signed about lowering the drinking age in the state. Luckily, he'd included his full address. That was easy. Anne used the maps program to route to his home. It wasn't that far from the hospital. After she dropped Ralph off, maybe she could just stop by.

Anne and Ralph ate a quick breakfast, and then she followed him to the mechanic shop in her car. As he chatted with Sal, a text came through. From Evelyn. ANNABELLE (LINDA'S DAUGHTER) IS COMING TO THE HOSPITAL AT 1 THIS AFTERNOON TO GET JOSHUA PALMER'S LETTERS. COME BY IF YOU WANT TO MEET HER.

Anne definitely wanted to meet her. I'LL BE THERE, she texted back.

Ralph hopped into her car, and they drove to the hospital together, listening to Ralph's favorite talk radio program. When they got there, she kissed him goodbye and he went off while she went to the Labor and Delivery ward. She walked directly up to the nurse's station and asked if anyone knew whether Dr. Lyle was working. Shirley had the day off, so Anne asked Paige, who shook her head.

"Haven't seen him, I'm afraid." Paige looked down the hallway. "I heard they're short-staffed over in orthopedic surgery," she said.

"We haven't had any C-sections this morning, so he might be over there."

Anne thanked her and made her way to the orthopedic ward to check, but the nurses there said Dr. Lyle wasn't around their floor either. Anne decided she would check in later, and she went to the volunteer room. Aurora assigned her to discharge, and that kept Anne busy for much of the morning. She planned to run a few errands on her lunch break, but before she left, she checked in at Labor and Delivery again to ask about Dr. Lyle.

"Turns out he's not coming in today," Paige said this time. "He had to take his family to the airport or something."

That was right. Brendan had mentioned that his wife and kids were going to visit Kate's family in Ohio. But hadn't he said the whole reason he couldn't go on the trip was because he had to work? He'd made it seem like he was working every day, but he'd taken the whole day off to take them to the airport?

"Oh." Anne tried to hide her disappointment—and her confusion. "All right then. Thanks for letting me know."

Anne went out to her car and followed the GPS directions to the apartment complex where Colton lived. It was an older brick place and a bit run-down, with a few old men sitting around on benches inside the lobby. There was a buzzer by the inner door, but the door hadn't closed all the way, so she pushed it open and crossed the lobby toward the elevator. This building must have been nice once, with its high molded plaster ceiling and the art deco trim. But the intervening years hadn't been kind, and the walls were painted a glossy sickly yellow and the brown floor tiles were dirty and cracked. The whole place had a skunky, musty smell.

Anne pressed the elevator call button, and a moment later the door opened, and a woman with three young children stepped out. Anne walked inside, pushed the button for floor 3, and held her breath as the door slid shut and the elevator creaked and groaned its way to the third floor. She stepped out and looked around for apartment 3C. The walls were the same awful yellow, and the doors were all an unfortunate shade of brown. She found apartment 3C around the corner, and she rang the doorbell and heard it echo inside the apartment. After a moment, there were footsteps, and then the door opened. A young woman—she couldn't be much more than twenty, if that—stood there with a newborn against her shoulder.

"Yes?" The girl's hair was in need of a wash, and she had dark circles under her eyes. She wore yoga pants and a stained oversized T-shirt. Ah, the blissful newborn phase.

"Hi. I'm looking for Colton Brown."

"He's out getting diapers."

"Do you know when he might be back?"

"He better he back soon." She narrowed her eyes at Anne. "Who are you?"

"I'm Anne Mabry. I'm from Mercy Hospital. We're looking into an incident that happened at the hospital on Monday, and I was hoping he might have some information."

"He had nothing to do with that," she said vehemently. "We already told the police that. We didn't even know it happened until you people came around asking about it. I need to go—"

She started to shut the door, but Anne put her hand on it. "I know he didn't have anything to do with it," Anne said. "He is not suspected of any wrongdoing. I was just hoping to talk to him because of a cell phone video."

"A cell phone video?"

"I was reviewing the security camera footage and saw Colton taking a video of the baby being wheeled to the nursery. I think there's a chance he may have caught a clue to the theft in the background of the footage. That's all," Anne said. "He's not a suspect in any way. I was just hoping I might be able to see that video."

The woman was still eyeing her skeptically. And probably rightly so, Anne reasoned. She was home alone with a newborn and Anne's story sure sounded a bit sketchy, at best.

"How about this? Can I leave my contact information with you?" Anne asked. "And if Colton would be willing to share the video with me, I would very much appreciate it. I would only use it for the purpose of trying to solve the theft on Monday, and again, Colton is not under any kind of suspicion himself."

The girl still looked skeptical, but she took Anne's information and promised to pass it on to Colton. Anne walked back to her car and thought for a minute about her next steps. She could—and probably should—head to the hospital. But there was another stop she wanted to make. It was probably a bad idea. It very well could get her in trouble. But still, Anne had a theory, and she knew she wouldn't stop wondering until she figured it out.

Anne typed the name CRESTVIEW into her GPS and started heading toward the nursing home on the west side. As she got closer, she tried to plan her strategy. How would she figure out if her theory was right? By the time she pulled into the parking lot behind the two-story brick building, she still didn't really have a plan. She would just see how it went.

Anne walked up to the door and was buzzed in, and then she asked the woman at the front desk where she could find Rick Martel.

"He's right down the hallway to your right. About halfway down." The woman was probably in her midforties, and she had a wedge haircut with blond highlights that stood out against her brown hair. "I'll just need you to sign in." She shoved a clipboard across the counter.

Oh dear. Anne understood why the home required visitors to register, but she had been hoping this was one of the places where security was a little more lax. But Anne took the pen and signed her name. Miranda would probably not be happy if she found out Anne had been here to see her father, but Anne would deal with that later.

She walked down the hallway to the right and searched for Rick's nameplate. There it was, as promised, about halfway down the corridor. Anne knocked gently on the door, which was pulled most of the way closed, and was greeted with silence.

"Hello?" Anne said softly. She pushed open the door and found a man sleeping in the hospital bed. The shades on the window were tightly closed, but a light was on at the far end of the room. A television on the dresser played a game show silently.

Given how much pain Anne had read that Rick was in, she was glad to see him resting comfortably now. And maybe it was better this way. What did she think was going to happen—that she would come in here and ask Rick if his daughter was slipping him painkillers she stole one or two at a time from the hospital? Even if she was right, and even if Rick knew about it, he was hardly likely to tell on his daughter, was he? Anne started to turn to go when a young woman in maroon scrubs appeared in the doorway of his room.

"Well, hello there," she said, her voice aggressively friendly. Her name tag read PRIYA CHIB. "I didn't know Rick had another visitor."

She spoke loudly, not even trying to keep her voice down, but Rick didn't stir.

"I'm a friend of his daughter's," Anne explained, though Priya hadn't asked.

"He'll be sorry he missed you. I'll make sure to tell him you stopped by."

Anne wasn't certain how to ask Priya not to do that.

"It's nice to see that he's sleeping so soundly," Anne said. She figured this was her one chance to see what she could find out. Might as well go for broke, since Miranda would probably discover she was here anyway. "I'd heard that he was in a lot of pain."

"Oh, he often is," Priya said. "But his daughter came this morning, and he often sleeps really well after her visits. I guess seeing her just wears him right out."

"Imagine that," Anne said as the pieces of the puzzle started to click into place. "He always feels better after Miranda sees him?"

"Like clockwork. I wish she would come visit more of our patients sometimes," Priya said with a laugh.

"How often does she come?"

"Every few days. It's nice that she's able to see him so often. So many of these patients, their families hardly ever come visit. But

Rick gets lots of attention from his daughter. We know it's about time for Miranda to come back when he starts complaining about being in pain again. And then, every few days, she shows up and his pain seems to disappear." She smiled like it was the most amazing thing.

Did she really not suspect? Anne wondered. Did no one at this nursing home wonder why Rick's pain got better after his daughter, a nurse at the hospital, came to visit? Or were they just looking the other way? Anne couldn't tell.

"He must be on a lot of pain medication," Anne said.

"Oh yeah, sure is, but the doctors here, they don't like to pre-scribe too much. They worry about getting sued if someone over-doses or something, I don't know. And the statistics on addiction are so scary, of course. But I'm kind of like, they're at the end of their lives anyway, why not let them feel good? I guess that's why I'm not a doctor." She laughed again. "But that's why it's so great how much seeing Miranda helps Rick. He just loves her so much, you know? It's so sweet to see."

It couldn't be a coincidence, Anne thought as she walked back to her car. That was what Miranda was doing with the pills she pil-fered from the Pyxis machines at the hospital. She wasn't working with Dr. Perez to get access to the medication and share kickbacks with her. She might be taking advantage of the large number of pre-scriptions for painkillers Dr. Perez wrote, but she wasn't then giving the stolen medication to the OB/GYN.

Miranda was taking one or two extra pills each time she accessed the painkillers in the machine, and she was giving them to her father to help relieve his constant pain from pancreatic cancer. It was sweet, and it was understandable. It was also dangerous and totally illegal. But Anne could see how she'd gotten there. When Ariane was in pain, her tiny body writhing in that big hospital bed, Anne would have done anything—really, pretty much anything—to take away her pain. She could understand why Miranda had been tempted to do the same for her father.

Anne would need to tell Garrison what she suspected. She didn't have any proof, but there was enough evidence in the Pyxis records to show a pattern of gross incompetence, if not willful theft. Anne supposed Miranda would be fired. The value of the medication Miranda had stolen no doubt amounted to grand theft. But Anne hoped they wouldn't press charges once they found out *why* she had been stealing the drugs. It was hard to fault her for the reason she had taken the medicine, no matter how wrong it was.

Still, did that mean Miranda had broken into the machine? Anne wasn't sure.

Chapter Thirteen

SHE REPLAYED THE INTERACTION WITH Amberlynn and the visit with Rick and the conversation she'd had with Dr. Lyle in her head as she drove back to the hospital. Had she misunderstood? Had he meant he'd had to work this weekend—Saturday and Sunday—but not Friday? Had he misspoken? Had his plans changed? Or was there more to it? Anne didn't want to be paranoid. Just because Dr. Lyle wasn't at work today didn't mean he had misdirected her. Not yet, anyway.

At one o'clock, Anne headed down to Records once more and found Evelyn and a woman with dark hair and big glasses inside the Vault.

"Anne, this is Annabelle, Joshua Palmer's great-great-granddaughter," Evelyn said. "Annabelle is a historian," she added, clearly pleased with this fact. "She teaches at South Carolina State."

"It's a pleasure to meet you," Anne said, holding out her hand. Annabelle was probably in her fifties, and she wore sensible slacks, flat-soled shoes, and a conservative button-down shirt. "Thank you so much for coming to get the letters."

"Are you kidding?" Annabelle said. "Thank you for finding them. You have no idea how much this means to our family."

"I'm sorry they don't contain better news about your ancestor," Evelyn said.

"I mean, obviously I wish he'd survived," Annabelle said. "But it was the not-knowing that made it so hard for his family. Just having the answers as to what happened, where he died and how—that's priceless to us. Obviously his wife and mother are long gone, but the family has always wondered. This will help."

"I'm so glad," Anne said.

"Were you able to determine why they were never mailed?" Annabelle asked. "Or how they ended up in this Vault?"

"I don't know," Evelyn said. "I wish I had answers for you, but I just don't. I suppose the mail was unreliable. Or maybe something happened to the nurse?"

"Well, in any case, I'm grateful that they were here," Annabelle said. "And that you tracked us down. You have solved a mystery that has plagued our family for generations. Thank you"

"We're happy to help." Evelyn met Anne's eyes, a smile on her face. "We quite enjoy solving mysteries around here."

Anne stayed later than usual, waiting for Ralph to finish up his shift, but thankfully he was able to duck out a bit early today, since he had to work tomorrow. Saturday shifts were unusual for him, but he had to cover for another chaplain who was on vacation. They were walking out to her car when her phone rang. It was an unfamiliar number, but a local area code. Anne decided to answer.

"This is Anne."

"Hi. This is Colton Brown. You came by my house this morning?"

"Colton. Thank you for calling me. First of all, congratulations on the new baby." Next to her, Ralph tilted his head, obviously curious who she was talking to.

"Thank you. He's pretty awesome."

"He looked adorable." Truthfully, all Anne had seen was the back of his head, but all babies were adorable, so she was confident in her words.

"Thanks." There was a pause. "So, Amberlynn said you asked about my cell phone video?"

"That's right," Anne said. "I think you're aware that there was a theft at the hospital Monday. A lot of dangerous medication was taken. You're not under suspicion of any kind, so please don't worry about that." She heard him let out a breath. "But in a security camera video I watched, I saw that you were in the hallway just outside the room where the theft occurred at approximately the right time. You were taking a video of the baby being wheeled to the nursery. I was hoping I could look at the video you took just to see if there were any clues."

"You want to use my video of my baby to see if there are any clues about a drug theft?" His voice was as skeptical as his words.

"I know it's a long shot," Anne said. "But we're trying to look at every angle just to make sure there's nothing we've missed. As you might imagine, the hospital is quite anxious to see this crime solved."

"Okay," he finally said. "This isn't going to be, like, broadcast or anything, right?"

"I promise we won't do anything of the sort with it," Anne said. "We'll just see if there are any clues to the theft in the background and leave it at that."

"All right," Colton said. "I guess I can email the video to you. Where should I send it?"

Anne gave him her email address, and he promised to send the video when he got off his shift later that evening.

She explained to Ralph as they drove home, and when they arrived at the house, Anne started working on dinner—baked macaroni and cheese. Anne hated to run the oven on a day as hot as this, but this dish had always been Lili's favorite. She cooked the pasta, layered it with the cheese, and slid it into the oven to bake.

When Lili and Addie arrived, Lili looked worn out from her week, and while Addie showed Ralph a YouTube video she loved about a guy who'd made a squirrel obstacle course in his backyard, Anne plied Lili with cheese and olives and tried to get her to open up.

"What are you doing at work these days?" Anne asked as she took the pasta out of the oven. The sauce was bubbling and the cheese on top was golden brown and crispy, exactly like she liked it.

"Just training," Lili said. "Standard stuff."

Okay, that didn't go as planned.

"How about your class? What are you working on there?"

"It's just introductory macroeconomics," Lili said. "We learned about supply chains this week. It's about as exciting as it sounds."

Anne had hoped Lili would show a little more enthusiasm for her introductory class, considering she was planning on earning a business degree. But it was Friday night, and Lili had to be exhausted. Anne decided to let her be while she finished up the salad and called everyone to the table.

After Ralph had prayed and the food had been served, Anne decided to broach the topic she'd been dreading head-on.

"I still haven't made any plans for our vacation yet," she said.

"Yikes, Anne. Don't you think we should make our reservations?" Ralph asked. "It's getting close."

Anne did think they should make reservations, very much so. She was trying. She tried to keep her voice calm as she continued.

"I have checked around at every possibility—from mountain cabins like you wanted"—she looked at Ralph—"to California like you wanted"—she glanced at Lili this time. "I've also researched beach houses, National Parks, and treehouses and yurts and pretty much everything in between."

"Yurts?" Ralph tilted his head.

"Are we going to Disney World?" Addie asked hopefully.

"I looked into Disney World too," Anne said. "And I can't seem to come up with anything that will make everyone happy." She took a deep breath. "At least nothing that's in the budget," she added, looking at Addie. "I'm not sure what to do, and I'm about ready to give up and say let's just do a staycation."

"Mom," Lili said, her eyes wide. "I didn't know you were so frustrated. I would have helped."

"You have enough going on," Anne said. "I didn't think it would be so hard to pick a place. But it turns out that none of you want to do the same thing." Anne was whining a little bit, she knew it, and she hated it. But she was so frustrated.

"We don't have to go to the mountains," Ralph said quickly. "That was just an idea. You asked for my thoughts, but that wasn't the only thing I'd be open to doing."

"And California was just a suggestion," Lili said. "It wasn't the only thing I was open to."

"You said you didn't want to go to the mountains."

"I said that was more Dad's thing. But I'm not against going there. I'm fine with anything."

"I'm fine with anything too," Ralph said. "And I'm happy to help with the research and booking. There's no reason for you to get so frustrated planning all of this. Why didn't you just ask for help?"

Anne didn't have an answer. She hadn't honestly considered asking Ralph for help because...well, when had he ever helped plan a vacation in the past? And because this was something she was supposed to do, wasn't it?

"I just wanted to find something that would make everyone happy," Anne said. "I wanted to make this vacation special."

"It *will* be special," Ralph said. "Because we'll all be together. It doesn't matter what we do."

"I disagree," Addie said. "I still want to go to Disney World."

Lili shushed her. "Really, Mom. Dad's right. It doesn't matter if we go to the beach or the mountains or Las Vegas or whatever."

"We're *not* going to Las Vegas," Ralph said.

Lili gave him a sly grin. She'd been teasing him. "The point is, we don't have to go somewhere fancy or spend a lot of money to have a good time on vacation. Some of my favorite vacations as a kid were the cheapest. I used to love when we went to that old campground over by the river. Remember that place?"

"The one with the playground with the creaky merry-go-round?" Anne remembered that now.

"And the showers that were always full of daddy longlegs," Lili added.

"You used to spend hours playing in the creek that ran through the property," Anne said, smiling at Lili.

"And I fished there. Caught dinner there most nights," Ralph said.

"Remember that one time the pop-up camper got a flat tire? Ralph asked. "And we weren't sure how we would get it out of there?"

"Whatever happened to that camper, anyway?" Lili asked.

"Oh, we sold it long ago," Ralph said, shaking his head. "I kind of wish we still had it, though."

"And remember that time the ants got into the food and we had to throw it all out and go into town and all we could find was canned vegetables?" Anne laughed, remembering how she'd tried to warm up canned green beans over the camp stove.

"We had some good trips there," Ralph said.

"Maybe we should just go there again," Lili said. "For old time's sake."

"We don't have the camper, though," Ralph said.

"I'm not sleeping in a tent," Anne said. "I'm too old to sleep in a tent."

"How hard could it be to borrow a camper?" Lili asked. "Dad, doesn't your friend Bill have one?"

"I guess he does," Ralph said, nodding. "I bet he'd let us borrow it. And we still have most of the equipment, but he could loan us whatever we don't have."

"That could be fun," Anne said. "Just like old times."

"It would be fun to introduce Addie to the wild world of camping, Mabry-style." Ralph grinned.

"You seriously want me to sleep outside?" Addie's eyebrows rose.

"Not under the stars, though that's fun too," Anne said. "In a camper. And there's a bathhouse with toilets and showers."

Addie still looked skeptical, but she was wise enough to keep it to herself.

"Camping certainly fits the budget," Ralph said. "God doesn't charge a penny to look up at that glorious night sky."

Once you added up the fuel and food and campsite fee and supplies, it wasn't exactly as close to free as Ralph was making it sound. But it was cheaper than a flight to California, that was for sure. And they would all be together, which was the main point. Most importantly, they all seemed excited about it. It was something they agreed on.

"There are some good trails near there, as I recall," Ralph said. "Didn't we hike to a waterfall once?"

"I don't know that I'd call it a waterfall," Anne said. "It was really just a trickle in the stream."

"I remembering it being big," Lili said. "I'd like to see it again. Let's do it. That would be fun." She turned to Addie. "I can't wait to show you this creek."

"I'll look into it," Anne said. "I'll check if they still have space left."

"See?" Ralph was smiling now. "That wasn't so hard, was it? We'll all be together."

"We could all be together at Disney World too," Addie said under her breath. Anne decided to let it pass. Once Addie saw how fun camping was, she would forget all about that mouse and his infernally expensive parks.

Anne realized she was smiling, already dreaming about what to pack and what to cook. Marshmallows, for sure, and graham crackers and chocolate. S'mores were a must. She needed to find the camp stove and the lantern. As she imagined it, she felt the first sense of peace she'd had while planning this trip all week. "This is going to be a great family vacation."

After Lili and Addie went home, Anne and Ralph cleaned up the kitchen and then, while Ralph got ready for bed, Anne checked her email one more time. Colton had said he would send the video when his shift was done. Was there any chance…

Aha. There it was. An email from Colton Brown.

> *Hi there. I think this is the video you were asking about. It's the only one I took in the hallway that day. I hope it gives you what you need.*
>
> *-C*

Below that was a video file. Anne clicked on it, and she watched as a nurse swaddled newborn Brady and laid him in the bassinet in the postpartum recovery room. The baby's mother—Amberlynn—was on the bed, a hospital gown slumping off her shoulders, her hair matted and messy.

"You'll bring him back soon?" she was saying.

"That's right," the nurse—it looked like Gina from this angle, but Anne wasn't sure—said in a soothing voice. "The doctor is just going to take a quick look at him to make sure he's healthy. We'll bring him right back."

"And you'll stay with him?" Amberlynn asked Colton.

"Of course I will. You just rest."

The nurse—it *was* Gina, Anne could see now—started pushing the bassinet, and Amberlynn blew kisses at the baby as he was wheeled off. Colton followed, keeping the camera focused on the moving bassinet.

"This is Brady's first trip to the nursery," Colton was saying in the video. "His first big trip. We're going to take you on so many trips, big guy." Colton had fallen a little behind, and he had to hurry to keep up with Gina. And in that few seconds while he was hurrying to catch up, the phone turned a bit, and the recovery room came into view at the back of the frame.

It was quick—just a glimpse into the right room at the right time—but it was enough. Anne gasped at what was going on inside.

Chapter Fourteen

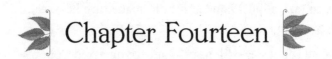

ANNE HATED TO INTERRUPT SHIRLEY'S Friday night, but she also knew Shirley had planned to go to dinner with Garrison, and Anne needed to talk to Garrison right away. She called her friend, and paced while it rang. Finally, just as Anne was about to give up, Shirley answered.

"Anne?"

"Shirley. I'm so sorry to bother you, but I need to talk to Garrison. Are you with him?"

"No, he dropped me off at home about twenty minutes ago. I'm just here with Mama. What's going on?"

"I know who did it. I have a video that shows the thief breaking into the Pyxis machine."

"Wait. What?" And then, a moment later, "Who is it?"

"I'm going to send it to you right now. I'm sending it to Garrison as well. Do you mind getting in touch with him and asking him to call me?"

"Not at all. Send it right away. I'll call Garrison right now."

Shirley hung up, and Anne kept pacing the kitchen, too keyed up to do anything else. A few minutes later, Shirley called back.

"Dr. Lyle? Really?"

She'd seen the video then. Seen the distinct shape of the doctor hunched over the machine, a long, thin metal strip in his hand, jimmying the drawers open.

"I know, it shocked me at first too." But then, as she'd thought about it while she was waiting for Shirley, it had started to make a strange amount of sense. Little things, clues she hadn't been able to fit anywhere, clicked into place. Loss of weight and change in sleep patterns were signs that someone was using.

Anne had the proof that cleared her name. She could show she hadn't been behind the theft. And yet she didn't feel vindicated. All she felt was sad.

"He was only in the room for a minute and a half, though," Shirley said.

"It didn't take him long to gain access," Anne said. "He knew where to find the ribbon retractor and how to use it to pry the drawer open. He runs marathons and works out—he's strong enough that it didn't give him much trouble. He knew which drugs were in the machine and where to find them."

"I just—" Shirley was quiet for a while, processing. "I didn't even take him seriously as a suspect. Not really."

"I didn't either, not at first. He didn't seem to really fit, did he? He's successful, handsome, charming, and rich. I know him, and I know his family. They've been members of St. Michael's forever and are respected in the community."

"It's always unwise to judge a book by its cover. Our other suspects had a lot of strikes against them," Shirley said, thinking it through. "Luke with his connection to the club, Olga with her history of addiction, Miranda with the irregularities in her history of using the machine. Dr. Perez, prescribing so many drugs."

"And we only saw the things that made those people look suspicious instead of taking a good hard look at our biases and assumptions. If we'd done that, the answer would have been right in front of us."

Dr. Lyle was one of the few who knew the drugs very well, and who knew where in the machine to find the ones he wanted. Miranda—the only other suspect who knew what the medications were and where to find them—had only ever taken Demerol, oxycodone, and hydrocodone in her own thefts. She had never taken fentanyl or hydromorphone. And Dr. Lyle was also the only suspect whose reputation and position within the hospital community allowed him to fly under the radar of their investigation. If only they hadn't been so dazzled by the front he presented to the world that they had been blinded to the truth lurking below the perfect surface.

Anne's phone beeped. She checked the screen.

"Shirley? Garrison is calling me."

"Answer it. And let me know what happens next."

"I will." She ended the call with Shirley and answered Garrison. "Hi, Garrison. Did you see the video?"

"I did. I don't know how you got it, but that was great work."

"Thank you," Anne said. "So what happens now? The evidence is pretty clear who it was."

"It is," Garrison said. "Sadly. I just—part of me can't believe it. Dr. Lyle, a drug addict? A drug supplier?"

Anne kept quiet, listening as he processed the news out loud. Inside, she was already moving on to worry—was Dr. Lyle selling the drugs? Was that part of how he funded his lavish lifestyle? Or was he so deep in addiction himself that he had been desperate enough to risk everything for quick access to the medication? That was how addiction often worked. You got to the point where you needed the drug so badly you'd put everything—your career, your family, your health—on the line to get it. You felt like you needed that next hit so badly that you didn't have a choice. Her heart ached, thinking about it. If Brendan had been desperate enough to really do this thing—and she had evidence he had—then he was already so far gone he was in deep trouble.

"I think we need to show the video to the police," Anne said. "I promised the guy who took the video we wouldn't put it online, but showing it to the police is something different."

Garrison sighed, and then he said, "You're right, of course. I'll forward it along now, and I'll give Detective Lee a call." He was hesitant, that was clear. But he would do it.

"I'm sorry," Anne said. "I know it's tough news to hear."

"It is, but I'm so grateful to finally know what really happened. Thank you for finding this, Anne."

"I'm just glad to help," Anne said. "Please keep me posted."

"I will."

Anne hung up, and when she turned around, she found Ralph standing in the doorway listening.

"It was Brendan?" he asked softly.

Anne nodded.

"That was what I was afraid of," Ralph said.

Ralph had known something. He'd known something, but he couldn't tell her. Anne wondered what had happened, what he knew about Brendan's past, but she also knew he would never tell her.

"I just wish I'd known." She didn't mean to pout. She wasn't upset at Ralph. She was just feeling blindsided.

"Would it have mattered, even if I had told you what I knew?" Ralph asked. "Would you have really suspected him?"

"Of course." But was that true? He'd definitely been one of the four people who had gone into that room, but even with that knowledge, she had never really treated him as a serious suspect. She'd been so focused on the others, who all seemed more likely. Looking back now, Anne realized how poorly she had judged each of the suspects. She had assumed Miranda had been stealing drugs to feed her own addiction, but in truth she'd been showing mercy to her poor pain-riddled father. She'd suspected Luke because of his past arrest, and—if she was honest—had probably let some of the strange tics he couldn't control cloud her judgment. She'd listened in disbelief as he told her that he'd gone into that room to check his stocks, because he didn't match her idea of someone who invested in and followed the stock market. She'd also looked at Olga and seen her past instead of who she truly was now.

Would Anne truly have seen who Brendan was, had she known? She honestly couldn't say. All she knew for sure was that she had judged many people incorrectly over and over during the course of this investigation.

"Let's get some rest," Ralph said, planting a kiss on her forehead. "Nothing new is going to happen tonight. You can check in in the morning."

Anne was too keyed up. She didn't feel like she could fall asleep anytime soon. But she followed Ralph to bed, and it didn't take long before she drifted off.

Ralph's car was still in the shop Saturday morning, and since he had to work, Anne got up early with him and took him to the hospital. As she drove, her mind kept replaying the footage she'd seen, and she wondered if the police had arrested Brendan yet or whether that would happen today. What was next for him? Would he have to serve time? She certainly hoped not. She hoped, instead, that he'd get sent somewhere he could be treated for…his addiction? Was he addicted? She assumed so. It made more sense than the idea that he had intended to sell the drugs—he clearly already had plenty of money—but she just wasn't sure.

She'd been thinking about Brendan so much on the drive that she was surprised to see him striding across the parking garage after she dropped Ralph off near the door to the walkway that connected the garage to the hospital. She blinked. Was that really him? She didn't trust her eyes for a moment. But she squinted, and there he still was, walking from the hospital toward his car, which she spotted down the row. She recognized it from his Instagram feed. He looked like he was just coming off a shift. Had he worked the night shift to make up for missing yesterday? In any case, he clearly hadn't been arrested. Were the police still gathering evidence? What was taking them so long?

Anne should just drive to the parking garage exit. She should take off and let the police do their work. She definitely should not get out of her car and go talk to the man she now knew had broken into the Pyxis machine. She shouldn't confront him and ask him what he'd been thinking. Her friends would caution her not to. Once he learned he'd been found out, it was hard to say what he would do. He could be dangerous.

But when she looked at him walking now, his scrubs wrinkled after a long night, his face tired, she didn't see an addict or a thief. What she saw was that little boy she'd known for so many years. He wouldn't hurt her—she believed that deep in her soul. He was hurting, and he needed help. So Anne ignored the voices telling her to stay in her car and drive away. Instead, she put her car into park, pushed open the door, and shouted, "Brendan!"

He turned, started, and narrowed his eyes. "Mrs. Mabry?"

She jumped out of the car and hurried to catch up with him. "Why did you do it?"

"What?" He shook his head. "Do what?"

"I know it was you. Why did you break into that machine?"

"I-I don't…," he stammered. He was looking at her like she was crazy. And, okay, she probably did seem kind of unhinged, accusing him in a parking garage, but she had to know why. Suddenly, she wanted to understand more than anything.

"It's on video, Brendan. I know you broke into that machine. I just want to understand." Oh dear. Probably she should have just kept her mouth shut and not told him about the video.

"You think *I* broke into the machine?" His voice didn't sound right, too high and brittle.

"We could have helped," Anne said. "Anyone at the hospital could have, or the church. We could have gotten you treatment. Or if you need money—if you thought you needed to sell—"

"I'm not selling drugs," he said, shaking his head. "I wouldn't—I never—"

"Did you take them for yourself? All those pills were for you?"

Brendan didn't respond her for a moment. He seemed to be trying to think of what to say. And then, instead of answering, he started walking toward his car again.

"We could have gotten you treatment," Anne repeated, pleading.

"If treatment worked, do you honestly think I'd be in this situation?" he yelled as he yanked open his door. "I've tried every kind there is. None of it helped."

And there it was. He had just admitted he was an addict, had basically just confessed to the theft. Anne expected to feel triumphant hearing that she'd been right, but really she just felt like she wanted to cry.

"If I can help—if I can do anything—"

Brendan didn't answer. He just got in his car, cranked the engine, and backed up. Anne watched as he drove away, speeding far too quickly in this garage. Would he be all right? When would the police come to arrest him? Anne didn't know, but she wished there was something she could do to help. At this point, all she knew to do was to pray. So she did, right there in that parking garage, asking God to help Brendan, and his family, through whatever was about to happen next. And then, finally, she got in her car and drove slowly back home, her heart heavy.

Anne spent the day cleaning, baking brownies for coffee hour at church the next day, and making a reservation at the campsite by the river. She was on edge all day, waiting for news, but none came. She tried calling Shirley, who was working at the hospital today, but the call went to voice mail. She dialed Ralph, but all he could tell her was that he didn't know what was happening. He hadn't heard anything from the police.

It was midafternoon by the time Shirley called her back.

"Sorry about that," Shirley said. "I was with a patient laboring, and the baby took her sweet time coming."

"That's okay. Did she have the baby?"

"A perfect little girl," Shirley said. "But what's going on? You sounded a bit…flustered in your message."

"Have you heard anything from Garrison about Brendan?"

"No. What about Brendan? Has he been arrested?"

"I don't know," Anne said. "That's what I'm trying to find out. He hadn't been this morning, when I saw him."

"You saw him?"

"In the parking garage, when I dropped Ralph off. He looked like he was done with his shift. I told him I knew it was him. I know I probably shouldn't have. I guess that's why I'm so anxious to know what's going on."

"Okay," Shirley said in her most soothing voice, and Anne realized she was starting to sound a bit crazy. "I'll call Garrison and see what I can find out. I imagine he turned your video over to the police and they're looking into it."

"I have a bad feeling," Anne said.

"The good news is, the police and the administrators are on it now, thanks to your help," Shirley said. "So it's off your plate."

"That doesn't mean I'm going stop worrying, at least not until Brendan is in custody and getting the treatment he needs."

"So you do think he took those pills for himself?"

"He basically admitted it to me," Anne said, and told her more about the confrontation in the parking garage that morning. "I probably shouldn't have confronted him. I just wanted to understand."

"Understand what? How desperate addiction can make someone?"

As she said the words, Anne realized again how silly her actions had been. She already knew how addiction changed people and made them do things they'd never imagine they would.

"You don't think he's going to do anything stupid, do you?" Shirley asked.

"I don't know," Anne said. "I mean, breaking into that machine in the first place was pretty stupid, so who knows what he might do now that he knows he's caught. He must have been pretty desperate already. And now... I don't know." She took a breath.

Anne sent a group text to Shirley, Joy, and Evelyn, giving the two others the update that she and Shirley already knew.

WHAT!? Joy wrote back immediately.

I DIDN'T SEE THAT COMING, Evelyn wrote. HE WAS LAST ON MY SUSPECT LIST. YOU'RE SURE?

I'M SURE, Anne replied.

JUST HEARD FROM GARRISON, Shirley texted the group. THE POLICE ARE TRYING TO GET A WARRANT BEFORE THEY GO TO DR. LYLE'S HOME, BUT THE JUDGE IS SICK, SO IT'S TAKING LONGER THAN USUAL. STILL TRYING. WILL KEEP YOU POSTED.

Anne wanted more than anything to go jump in and do something—talk to the police, ask whether he'd been arrested yet, or research drug treatment facilities—but she had already done enough. She needed to stay out of the way and let the police do their job.

Her job now was also to keep praying. She prayed for wisdom to know what to do and for patience as she let the police work. She prayed for Brendan, that this tragic theft might finally be the impetus for him to get the help he needed. She prayed for Kate and the kids, as the family dealt with the aftermath of whatever was to come. No matter what happened next, they had many difficult days ahead. She prayed for Greg and Charlotte and for the whole Lyle family. But mostly she prayed for Brendan, that the Lord would help and protect him and guide him through the dark days ahead.

Anne was so absorbed in prayer that she almost didn't recognize the sound of her phone bleating from the far end of the table. She opened her eyes and reached for it and saw that it was Ralph calling.

"Hello?"

"Anne, could you come pick me up?"

"Of course." His shift wouldn't be over for a few hours, but she could tell by the tone of his voice and the shortness of his words that this was important. He was in a hurry. "Why?"

She was already grabbing her purse and slipping on her shoes as he explained. "I just got a call from Charlotte Lyle. She told me she'd gotten a strange message from Brendan. His words were slurred, and he sounded out of it. He said something about the police and how sorry he was. She thought he—well, he'd been high on something, that was pretty clear to her. She said he wasn't making a lot of sense. And she has a bad feeling, but she and Greg are in Italy at the moment, so they asked me to go over and check on him."

If only Ralph's car wasn't in the shop! Brendan's home wasn't far from the hospital. Ralph would be able to get there so much quicker if he didn't have to wait for her to drive in first. "I'm on my way. I'll be there as soon as I can."

Anne hopped in her car, and at the first stoplight, she used voice-to-text to send a message to her friends about what was going on and letting them know she was about to take Ralph over to check on Brendan. Then she drove as quickly as she dared to the hospital, praying the whole way. When she was almost there, she got a text from Ralph that simply said, I'LL BE AT THE BACK ENTRANCE. A few minutes later, she pulled up at the spot where she usually discharged patients, and Ralph was there and so was Shirley.

"When I got your message, I tracked Ralph down," Shirley said as they both climbed into the car. "Just in case."

She didn't need to say in case of what. Anne knew what Charlotte suspected and why she'd asked Ralph to go to his house. She worried Brendan was using, had taken more than he should have—either as an accidental overdose or something worse, she wasn't sure. But she guessed Charlotte was hoping they could help in case Brendan needed it. As long as they weren't too late.

Ralph gave her Brendan's address, and she plugged it into her phone and they set off. He lived on Murray Boulevard, just a few blocks from the hospital. They'd be there soon.

Chapter Fifteen

ANNE WAS FILLED WITH UNEASE as they pulled up in front of the house a few minutes later. It was a beautiful raised three-story home with three porches overlooking the Ashley River and the Charleston Harbor. It was not too far from the hospital, which no doubt made for an easy commute. The small front yard was beautifully landscaped, with palmetto trees framing the front door, and the house itself was painted a soft sage green with white trim and black shutters. Anne found a parking spot on the street, and they all climbed out.

There were two cars in the driveway. Two very nice cars. Brendan's sporty BMW sat on the thin strip of pavement that ran alongside the house, with a silver Range Rover behind it. The Range Rover had stick figure stickers representing the family on the back window. Kate's car, most likely.

"Someone's home," Shirley said.

"Maybe," Anne said. "The BMW is his. If he really did take his wife to the airport yesterday, the other one could be hers."

"Let's go see," Ralph said. He strode up to the porch and rang the doorbell. "Brendan?" A newspaper in a filmy blue bag sat on the porch. They waited, but there was no answer. No movement inside. Ralph rang it again, and then, when there was still only silence, pounded on the door with his fist. "Brendan!"

Anne's unease had begun to turn to dread. Something wasn't right here. "Should we go around to the back?"

"I think we'd better," Ralph said. They stepped off the porch. "Why don't you two wait here, and I'll go see?"

"No way. I'm coming too," Anne said.

"We don't know what the situation inside is," Ralph said. "He may be inside. He may be dangerous, if he thinks he's about to be caught."

"All the more reason for us to come with you. You can't face him alone."

Maybe Ralph was worried about that too, or maybe he had other ideas about what was really happening inside, but he didn't argue, and Anne and Shirley followed him around the side of the house. Anne stopped and peeked in a window. The kitchen. A huge marble island, a large silver sink, a professional-looking range, two fridges and a double oven. But no people, no movement. They kept walking, squeezing past the cars in the narrow driveway, and came to the backyard, surrounded on three sides by a brick wall covered in wisteria and honeysuckle vines. There was a small patch of grass, a built-in grilling station and pizza oven, and a patio with wrought iron table and chairs. A glass door led into the house. Anne walked up to the door and knocked on the frame, three loud knocks. Once again, there was no movement and no answer. Anne peered in. This was a dining area, with a long Scandinavian-design table and chairs in front of a wall covered with what looked like colorful updated Victorian wallpaper.

Ralph knocked on the back door again and was greeted by silence. "Brendan!"

"It looks like he's not here," Shirley said.

"He's here." Anne put her hand on the doorknob. "I think we should go in."

"Normally, I wouldn't be in favor of just entering someone's home," Ralph said. "But under the circumstances…"

"Charlotte asked you to check on him, right?" Anne asked.

"She did." Ralph nodded. "In case he…" He couldn't seem to make himself say the words.

"Let's go, then," Anne said.

"Better let me go first," Ralph said, and Anne stepped aside. Ralph turned the doorknob and pushed gently, and the door swung inward. He walked inside, and Anne was only a step behind him.

"Dr. Lyle?" she called. Her words echoed in the still home.

"Brendan?" Ralph called from in front of her. "It's Ralph Mabry."

"Brendan?" Anne tried again. "Are you here?"

Ralph crossed the dining area into the kitchen, with Anne and Shirley just a step behind. There were dirty plates in the sink. An empty water glass. But he wasn't here. Anne walked through the kitchen, past an empty pantry that was the size of her own kitchen, past a bathroom, and into…was it a library? There was a desk, a few club chairs, a banker's lamp, and bookshelves lining the walls. But none of that was what had caught Anne's attention.

"In here," Anne said. "Brendan!"

Shirley must have seen what Anne did. She rushed ahead.

"Brendan!" Ralph called again, louder this time.

But the body that lay still behind the desk didn't move.

Chapter Sixteen

SOMETHING WAS VERY, VERY WRONG, that much was immediately clear. Brendan's body lay still, crumpled at an odd angle at the foot of the desk. There were no visible wounds, and no blood, but his skin was very pale, with a bluish tinge. A shattered coffee cup and a puddle of coffee rested on the wood floor. His breathing was shallow and labored, but he was breathing. *Please, Lord, don't let us be too late.*

Kneeling at her side, Shirley assessed him. "This has all the signs of an overdose," she said, digging in her purse. "Call 911."

Anne was already pulling her phone out of her pocket and dialing. Shirley drew a plastic tube out of her purse. It looked like a nasal spray. Narcan. Thank God Shirley had come. Shirley shook the bottle and administered the spray.

"Come on, now," she said. "Breathe it in."

"911, what's your emergency?"

"We have suspected overdose," Anne said. She gave the address, and the dispatcher promised to send an ambulance right away. Shirley pressed her fingers to Dr. Lyle's neck, searching for a pulse.

"The ambulance is on the way," the dispatcher said.

"My friend is a nurse. She administered Narcan," Anne said.

"Then she's doing everything right," the dispatcher said. "Just hang on. Help will be there shortly." Anne could actually hear the sirens as they whipped through the narrow cobblestone streets toward the house. "Just hang on the line."

As she waited, watching Shirley do her very best to bring Dr. Lyle back from the brink, all Anne could do was pray.

Please, Lord, she prayed. *He has young children. They need him.*

Please, Lord. He has an illness. Let him survive and get treatment.

Please, he has a mother who loves him more than life itself. Please don't break his mother's heart.

Ralph had his head bowed, his hand on Brendan's. Clearly he was praying as well.

In those tense moments, it didn't matter that he was a thief and an addict. It didn't matter that he was the person Anne had been searching for all week and who had lied to her face. All that mattered was that he was a child of God, and he needed help.

As she heard the sirens pull up in front of the house, Anne ran to the front door and unlocked it before, throwing it open. Moments later, the EMTs rushed inside, a stretcher carried between them. Anne didn't recognize the paramedics, but she did recognize the logo on the pocket of their scrubs. The angel logo of Mercy Hospital had never looked sweeter.

"They're here," she said into the phone.

Anne had been around medical emergencies before, but she was still surprised by how quickly and efficiently the paramedics got

Brendan on oxygen and loaded onto the stretcher and out the door. When the paramedics were gone and only Anne, Ralph, and Shirley were left in the house, they looked at one another.

"Well, it seems Charlotte was right," Ralph said, his voice defeated. He appeared as if he was about to cry. Anne rarely saw him get emotional like this. She pulled him in for a hug, and Ralph hugged her right back.

"Will he be all right?" Anne asked Shirley, finally pulling away. Her tough-as-nails friend looked shell-shocked.

"I don't know. I hope so. But there's no telling how long he'd been here like that. It could have been many hours." Anne nodded. She remembered from Nick's most recent overdose that it wasn't often a quick process. But she knew that if someone intervened in time, there was hope. And Shirley had intervened.

"But he was in a bad way," Shirley continued.

"Thank goodness you had the Narcan."

"The naloxone was the most important thing," Shirley said. "It can save lives. Let's hope it did the trick in this case." She sighed and gestured down at the mess on the floor. "How about we clean this up, and then we can go back to the hospital and check on him?"

"I'm going to go make a call first," Ralph said.

Anne guessed that he was going to call Brendan's mother to tell her the news. This was going to be one of the hardest phone calls he'd ever made in his life. But she also knew how much comfort it would give Charlotte to know that they had arrived in time and that it might not be too late.

Chapter Seventeen

LATER THAT AFTERNOON, ANNE, SHIRLEY, Evelyn, and Joy were gathered in the garden in Joy's backyard, drinking iced tea. A soft breeze stirred the sultry air, and bumblebees floated around the hibiscus and hydrangea blooms. Black-eyed Susans, purple coneflowers, dahlias, and camelias made the garden bright and cheerful, and the wrought iron table in the shade of the house was cool. Anne and Shirley filled Joy and Evelyn in on what had happened that morning.

"So he's okay?" Joy asked, her eyes wide.

"He's conscious, and he seems like he's going to be all right," Shirley said. "It's too early to say for sure. The last thing he remembers is walking into that library with his morning coffee, so it was probably hours that he was there. He'd taken fentanyl, but there were traces of other drugs in his system as well. He must have taken several different kinds of medication over the past few days."

"Including twice the usual dose of fentanyl, apparently," Anne added. "Though he says it wasn't on purpose. He says the stress of the situation drove him to find relief, and he took more than usual."

"The stress of being found out after he'd stolen thousands of dollars' worth of narcotics?" Evelyn asked wryly.

"He's an addict," Anne said gently. "It's no excuse, but—well, he wasn't thinking rationally, I'm sure."

"The important thing is that they predict he'll make a full recovery," Shirley said.

"It will be a while before they know if any damage was done, but Dr. Barnhardt was hopeful," Anne added. "And it's all because of Shirley's quick thinking."

"There was no thinking involved," Shirley said. "My training kicked in and took over. And it was really the Narcan that did it."

"They said that if Shirley hadn't administered the Narcan when she did, he probably wouldn't have made it," Anne said.

"And I wouldn't have been there to administer the Narcan if you hadn't figured out it was Brendan." Shirley elbowed Anne.

"Or if he hadn't called his mother, slurring his words and making no sense," Anne said. "That's what made her reach out Ralph to ask him to check on Brendan."

"It's really fortunate that she called Ralph when she did," Evelyn said.

Anne took a sip before answering. "I don't think fortune had anything to do with it. I think God was working to make sure we got there in time."

"Amen," Joy said.

"Well, God used your good sense in tracking down that video," Shirley added.

They all laughed again. The tea was cold, and it felt refreshing on this steamy summer day. Shirley was right, but Anne had also seen God work in miraculous ways throughout her time at the hospital. As far as she was concerned, this was just another one of those times.

And to think that she'd almost missed it. She'd been so distracted by Brendan's accomplishments and reputation and her relationship with his family that she'd failed to see what was right there in front of her all along. She of all people should have known that addiction can affect anyone, anywhere, and that what you see on the surface is not always what's really going on. Only the Lord knew what was in people's hearts, and a good front could distract even the most clever sleuths from discerning the truth.

Anne's cheeks burned when she thought of the other ways she'd misjudged people in the course of this mystery. She'd misread just about every suspect she'd encountered throughout the week. She'd allowed preconceptions, rumors, and her own biases to get in the way of seeing the truth. *People look at the outward appearance, but the Lord looks at the heart.* After so many years in ministry, how did she not know better? But she supposed she would always have to work at it, and with the Lord's help, she may get there one day.

"I imagine Dr. Lyle won't be working as an anesthesiologist at Mercy for a while," Joy said.

"I imagine not," Evelyn said. "Or any hospital for that matter, even after the legal issue is settled."

"I'm sure he'll be in treatment for quite some time," Shirley said.

"Let's pray it helps." Anne understood the statistics and how difficult it was to break free from addiction. She knew recovery was a lifelong struggle. But she also believed that God was powerful; He was the breaker of bonds. "I'll be praying for him."

"But he wasn't the last person who went into that recovery room," Joy said. "Both Luke and Olga went in there after he'd pried the machine open. Did they really just…not see the damage?"

"Both of them told me they didn't," Anne said. "Olga was too distracted by what was going on with her son. And Luke said he never noticed the Pyxis machines at all or knew what they were called."

"And I guess we should believe them," Shirley said. "No matter how strange that sounds."

"So Dr. Perez"—Evelyn shook her glass gently, allowing the ice to resettle—"didn't have anything to do with it?"

"Apparently not," Anne said. "I told Garrison that we'd been looking into her, and they're aware that she writes a large number of prescriptions. But as far as anyone can tell, she doesn't seem to benefit from them in any way."

"Maybe she owns stock in one of the big pharmaceutical companies," Evelyn said in her typical dry tone.

"That would be a roundabout way to increase her net worth, I suppose," Joy said, shaking her head. "But probably not something the hospital is going to be investigating themselves."

"Not anytime soon," Anne said.

"What about Miranda?" Joy took another sip of her tea. "What's going to happen to her?"

"She's being let go, from what I understand," Shirley said. "She's confessed. And even though Anne discovered she stole the medication for compassionate reasons, she was still stealing expensive drugs."

"Not to mention, she put her father in danger," Evelyn said. "Slipping him extra medicine on top of what he had been prescribed could have had disastrous consequences."

"I feel for her, though," Anne said. "Watching someone you love suffer so much...is extremely painful—for both of you." Anne hadn't meant to get choked up, but her voice still broke as she spoke.

Without a word, Joy reached out and put her hand on top of Anne's and gave it a squeeze. No doubt they all guessed Anne was thinking about Ariane. It was true. Anne would have done anything to help her daughter. But she couldn't—no one could. All she'd been able to do was trust that God was in control, no matter what. Even when people you loved more than life itself didn't make it. Even when people you loved struggled, making bad decisions and throwing away everything they cherished because of the handcuffs of addiction. Even when you saw how thin the line between life and death truly was. Even then, God was in control of the world He had made.

No one said anything for a moment.

"I'm glad you're going to get to spend some good time with your family in a few weeks," Joy said. "That will be a nice break, after all this."

"I am too," Anne said. "Now that I'm not stressing about where we're going, I'm really looking forward to it. It will be nice to just enjoy the time we have together."

"Enjoy them while you can," Shirley said quietly.

"Make those memories." Joy smiled.

"And who knows, now that this mystery is solved, maybe things will be quiet for a little while," Evelyn said.

"I don't know." Joy took a sip and looked at them all over the rim of her glass. "I wouldn't count on it. Somehow these mysteries seem to find us."

They laughed once more, and Anne sat back and looked around at her friends gathered together around the table. She didn't know what tomorrow would bring. Maybe another mystery, some life-changing news, or—God forbid—tragedy. All she could do was trust in God and enjoy each day the Lord gave her.

She couldn't wait to see what He would do next.

Dear Reader,

My mom likes to tell me that when she and her sister were growing up, there were two career paths available to women—they could be a nurse or they could be a teacher. My mom became a teacher; her sister, my aunt Mary, became a nurse. Aunt Mary spent her career as a labor and delivery nurse, providing a steady hand and caring words as she helped coax new life into the world, day after day. My aunt never had children of her own, but she never tired of seeing the miracle that is a baby. I imagine many nurses would lose some of their sense of wonder after a while—birth is a life-changing miracle to the baby's parents, after all, but to the hospital staff, they see it dozens of times a day. But my aunt always took pride in giving the best care possible to the women in her charge.

When I was finishing up my first book in this series, I called my aunt to check some details about how hospitals work, and when I told her I was thinking about ideas for a new book in this series, she had a few suggestions. She told me about a famous nurse who killed hundreds of his patients (too dark), about a famous kidnapping from the hospital nursery (it's been done), and about an anesthesiologist she worked with who once broke into a Pyxis machine and cleaned it out. I had no idea what a Pyxis machine was or why an anesthesiologist would need to break into one. But as she explained what had happened—why he chose the machine in the C-section recovery room, how he broke in, why he wanted to get into the machine without leaving a record—this story started to take shape. I learned so much about how hospitals manage medication and about how dangerous the medication can be when it's abused.

The opioid crisis in our country is real, and it's escalating. Narcan—the nasal spray Shirley uses to revive Dr. Lyle in this book—is real and can help save lives. If you or someone you know uses opioids, please think about getting a prescription to carry it. And if you or anyone you know needs help dealing with an addiction, there is help. You can call the National Substance Abuse and Mental Health Services Administration's helpline (1-800-662-4357) 24/7 for treatment referral and information.

Signed,

Beth Adams

About the Author

BETH ADAMS LIVES IN BROOKLYN, New York, with her husband and two young daughters. When she's not writing, she spends her time cleaning up after two devious cats and trying to find time to read mysteries.

An Armchair Tour of Charleston

IN THIS BOOK, JOSHUA PALMER is a Union soldier injured at the Battle of Fort Sumter and later treated at Mercy Hospital. The Battle of Fort Sumter, as Anne shares in this book, was the battle that started the Civil War.

Construction of Fort Sumter began in 1829 as part of a series of forts designed to defend the American coastline. After president Lincoln was elected in 1860, South Carolina seceded from the Union, and several other Southern states followed to form the Confederate States of America.

However, American troops still guarded Fort Sumter, even as Confederate forces within Charleston—the city the fort was designed to protect—declared the Union troops were illegally occupying land they now claimed. On April 12, 1861, the Confederate Army attacked Fort Sumter, setting off the first in a long string of bloody battles that reshaped American history. After the Confederate Army's surrender in 1864, the American flag was once again raised over Fort Sumter, and the fort continued to be used by the military through World War II.

Today, Fort Sumter is a National Historical Site, and you can take a short ferry ride to visit it from Charleston. See history come alive on this little island that started it all.

Good for What Ails You

LILI'S FAVORITE BAKED MACARONI AND CHEESE

Ingredients:

1 pound elbow macaroni

2 cups milk (whole, preferably)

2 large eggs

4 cups shredded extra-sharp cheddar (about 16 ounces), divided

½ cup unsalted butter, melted

1 ½ teaspoons salt

½ teaspoon pepper

2 cups Colby Jack cheese (about 8 ounces), grated and divided

Directions:

1. Preheat oven to 350. Salt a large pot of water and bring it to boil. Add macaroni and cook according to package directions. Drain and rinse.

2. In a large bowl, whisk milk and eggs. Add cooked macaroni, 2 cups extra-sharp cheddar, melted butter, and about 1½ teaspoons salt and ½ teaspoon pepper and mix well.

3. Add half the macaroni mixture to a greased 9×13-inch baking dish. Spread 1 cup Colby Jack cheese on top. Spread

remaining macaroni mixture on top. Cover with foil and bake for 30 minutes.

4. Remove from oven. Carefully lift foil and top macaroni with remaining 2 cups cheddar and 1 cup Colby Jack. Broil until cheese is melted and browned in spots, about 3 to 5 minutes.

5. Remove from oven and let rest for about 15 minutes before serving.

Read on for a sneak peek of another exciting book
in the Miracles & Mysteries of Mercy Hospital series!

Redeemed by Mercy
by ELIZABETH PENNEY

EVELYN PERRY SET A FRAMED oil portrait into place. "Ladies, I present to you Dr. Walter Waring, one of Mercy's first doctors and a good friend of our founder, Doc Fleury." During her Friday lunch hour, Evelyn was working on an exhibit in the hospital's new museum. Her best friends, who served at Mercy as well, had popped by to check out her progress.

Anne Mabry cocked her head to take in the painting, which depicted a whiskered man wearing a black wool suit, a pince-nez perched on his formidable nose. "He's very distinguished looking. Quite intimidating."

"I wonder what his bedside manner was like," Joy Atkins said with a chuckle.

"Not good, I'm guessing. Ask me how I know." Shirley laughed, and the others joined in. Since Shirley rotated nursing shifts in different departments, she worked with many of the doctors, and she definitely had her favorites.

As Evelyn moved to the next portrait, Joy said, "You must be excited about your vacation."

"I sure am," Evelyn said. "It starts tonight, with the cookout at our house. Y'all are coming, right?" As they each confirmed, Evelyn realized how excited she was about taking two whole weeks off. She felt as giddy as a child on the last day of school.

"What are your plans?" Anne asked. "Do you have a schedule?" This comment was a teasing reference to Evelyn's love of organization.

She laughed. "I don't, believe it or not. This all started with James agreeing to work in Isle of Palms for the *Celestial* shipwreck project this summer. I thought I'd take the opportunity to tag along part of the time."

A salvage company had hired Evelyn's history professor husband to identify and log seventeenth-century artifacts, which was a dream job for him. The *Celestial* had sunk offshore during the big hurricane of 1720, near Isle of Palms, South Carolina, a quaint vacation community. He and Evelyn had booked a room close to the project headquarters and across the street from the beach.

"You'll have to chill while he's cataloging," Shirley said. "Sit back. Relax. Do absolutely nothing."

Evelyn snorted, joined by similar scoffing noises from Anne and Joy. "I'll try," she said. "You know me."

Anne had wandered to a nearby glass case holding vintage medical equipment. "We'll come over and make you," she said. "Force you to sit on the beach."

Evelyn perked up at this idea. "I hope you do visit me. I don't think I can go two whole weeks without seeing y'all."

"Will James mind?" Joy asked. "I'm sure he's looking forward to getting you all to himself."

"Oh, we'll have plenty of couple time," Evelyn said. "Which, to be honest, I can't wait for. Thirty-five years of marriage and he's still my favorite person. Not to slight y'all," she added.

Shirley sighed. "I love hearing that. Maybe someday…" Shirley had been dating Garrison Baker, Mercy's hospital administrator, since the beginning of the year, and from what Evelyn knew, things were going very well.

Joy's smile was a little sad. "Savor the moments. I did, and I'm so thankful now." Joy had lost her husband a couple of years ago, which had prompted her move from Texas to Charleston to live near her daughter.

"I try to, every single day. I do wish we could have met Wilson." Evelyn glanced up when two women appeared in the museum doorway, where they hovered. One clutched a fat manila envelope. "Please feel free to come in and browse around," she called. Usually volunteers staffed the space, but she'd sent today's volunteer off to have lunch while she was working.

Anne crossed the room to greet the women. "Clara. Alice. I'm so glad you could make it." She escorted them over to where Evelyn was standing. "Evelyn, I'd like you to meet Clara Waring Aiken and Alice Waring. This is Evelyn Perry, who came up with the idea for this museum."

"Nice to meet you." Evelyn glanced at the first portrait. "Descendants of Walter?"

"Yes, we are," Clara said. Her eyes were striking, one blue and the other brown. "Alice is my sister. But we're actually here about an even earlier ancestor, Dr. Samuel Waring. He opened his practice in 1715, which makes him one of Charleston's first doctors. We were hoping you could include him in the exhibit."

"When I heard about Samuel, I thought he might be a perfect fit, Evelyn," Anne said. "He has such an interesting story." She gestured toward Alice. "Alice told me about him when I was signing Addie up for the summer program at the Waring School." Anne and her husband, Ralph, cared for their eight-year-old granddaughter when their daughter was on duty or deployed with the military. Right now Lili was away taking a multiweek course. "The *Celestial* project is one of their focus areas this year."

"It is a fascinating story," Evelyn said. She waved goodbye to Joy and Shirley, who were slipping out of the museum to go back to work. "The Waring School has been around for a long time, hasn't it?"

"Since 1725," Alice said. "Samuel and his wife, Jane Middleton Waring, were the founders. It was a full-time school until the early 1900s, when they started offering short-term educational programs for children in history, science, and the arts, all with a local focus."

Clara took up the tale. "Jane, who was on her way to Boston to become a governess, survived the shipwreck of the *Celestial*. She married Samuel here in Charleston, and the rest is history. In his diary, Samuel talks about the mission to rescue Jane and how he cared for her after her ordeal." She held out the manila envelope. "I have it here, if you'd like to read it."

A diary from the early 1700s? Evelyn's heart skipped a beat. *I really am a history nerd*, she thought as she accepted the envelope. Since Samuel's diary touched on the shipwreck, she was sure James would be interested as well.

"If you decide to include him," Clara said, "we have his ledgers, some other papers, and a medical bag. We'd be happy to lend anything you want for the exhibit."

"That would be very generous of you," Evelyn said. While the hospital vault had provided some information and artifacts, a significant number of exhibit materials were on loan from family members.

"Oh, and one more thing. We have a portrait of Samuel and Jane with their firstborn, Walter's great-grandfather," Clara said. "Show them, Alice."

She took out her phone and scrolled, then held the screen so they could see it. The portrait showed an attractive young couple, the woman seated and holding a baby. She had one light eye and one dark eye.

Clara said, "Do you notice her eyes? That's called heterochromia. It's a symptom of Waardenburg Syndrome, which runs in our family." She patted her dark hair, which had a prominent white streak in front. "This is another symptom."

"Passed down from Jane," Alice said. "Clara is only thirty-five."

"It looks good on you," Evelyn said. Clara's white streak was distinctive, especially with those unusual eyes. "This is all very intriguing. I hate to say this, because he obviously was a wonderful doctor, but Samuel's story doesn't really fit this exhibit. He never worked at Mercy. He couldn't have, because the hospital wasn't built yet."

Clara seemed ready for this objection. "The Waring family was a big contributor to the building of the hospital, at the request of Doc

Fleury," she said. "Doctors in our family worked here from the beginning. Without Samuel, none of that would have happened."

She had a point. Evelyn racked her brain trying to figure out if she should extend the exhibit scope to pre-Mercy doctors when Stacia Westbrook, her assistant, rushed into the room. She stopped short when she saw the Waring sisters with Evelyn and Anne. "Oops, I'm sorry. I didn't mean to interrupt." She waved the phone she held. "But Evelyn, James is going to be on the local news, talking about the shipwreck."

"James is my husband," Evelyn told Clara and Alice. "Come join us, Stacia. We want to watch with you." Evelyn was a little miffed that James hadn't told her about the newscast. But then she patted her pockets and realized she'd left her phone on her desk in the records department.

Stacia trotted over to the group and positioned herself in the middle. "Here it comes." She turned up the volume.

"Today a company salvaging artifacts from the schooner *Celestial* made an exciting discovery," Bailey Carver, a local newscaster, said. Bailey stood on a harbor dock, and the chyron read, "Isle of Palms Discovery."

The camera swung to show the water and then back to the newscaster, with two men in the frame—James and a tall, balding man with a big mustache whom Evelyn recognized as W. Deacon Stokes, head of the salvage company. Everyone called him by his last name.

"Stokes, tell us about your find," Bailey said.

"As you know," he said, "we've been working to salvage as much as we can from the *Celestial*, which sank in 1720. The *Celestial* was carrying cargo and a few passengers from Barbados to Boston. We've found some wonderful stuff so far, and I can't wait to share it with the public. Today, though, our crew brought up something totally unexpected." He paused dramatically. "A second ship's hull. We think it might be the *Hannah B*, which, legend has it, sank during the same storm. We also believe it's from the *Hannah B* because the ship was spotted lurking in the Outer Banks before the storm. And afterward? Never seen again."

"And that is significant why?" Bailey asked.

Now James spoke. He looked very handsome, with his thick, dark hair and distinguished beard. "The *Hannah B* was a pirate ship. No one was ever sure what happened to it or the crew until now. By the looks of the debris field, the pirate ship may well have been confronting the *Celestial* when the storm hit. The two ships' remains are mingled, we think."

"The *Hannah B* was robbing the *Celestial*, you mean?" Bailey asked, her eyes wide.

"Yes, exactly," James said. "The *Hannah B* was notorious for the ruthless and daring attacks carried out by her crew. The most famous pirate on board was a woman, Polly O'Brien. Along with the ship, she dropped out of sight in 1720."

Someone gasped, and when Evelyn glanced at the others, she saw that they looked as amazed as she felt. Retrieving artifacts from a shipwreck was exciting enough, but the involvement of a pirate ship put a whole new angle on the story. At that time, pirates—including the most famous, Blackbeard himself—had terrorized the Carolina coast and beyond. Female pirates were quite rare, with only a handful known to history. Evelyn sometimes wondered what would spur a woman to become an outlaw so reviled that, if caught, she would hang.

"We think now that Polly must have gone down with her ship," Stokes said. "Hopefully we will find artifacts that shed light on her life and those of her partners in crime."

"How exciting," the newscaster said. "People find pirates so interesting, although I'm sure they were feared at the time."

"Very much so," Stokes said.

"We look forward to hearing more," Bailey said. "Thank you both."

With that, the broadcast cut to another story, this one featuring windsurfing at the beach. Not something Evelyn wanted to try during her vacation, she thought ruefully.

"That was amazing," Stacia said with a sigh. "I wonder what they'll find next. Treasure, maybe?" The phone rang across the hall, and she sprang into action. "I'd better get that. I'm expecting a call back." With a wave, she trotted away.

"I'll be in shortly," Evelyn promised. Her lunch hour was almost over.

"I should get going too," Anne said. "Flower deliveries upstairs." As a volunteer, Anne enjoyed dropping off the bouquets ordered from the gift shop. She often found opportunities to get to know, comfort, and pray with patients.

"I'll go with you," Alice offered. "You said in your phone message that you had questions about the school schedule?"

"Yes, I do," Anne replied. "Want to walk and talk?"

That left Evelyn alone with Clara. "Do you mind if I share Samuel's diary with my husband?" Evelyn asked. "You said Samuel helped with the rescue, so I'm thinking there might be some good background information in there." After hearing the news story,

Evelyn was curious herself and also wondering if Jane, the rescued passenger, had ever said anything about encountering Polly O'Brien. They might have to dig beyond the diary to find out.

"Of course not," Clara said. Her eyes were bright with excitement. "Did you know about the pirate ship going down with the *Celestial*?"

Evelyn shook her head. "Today was the first I heard of it. I don't think James and the salvage company had any idea until they found the other ship's hull." With the way artifacts were covered with sand and silt, it was a miracle anything was ever discovered.

Clara moved closer. "I just had the most outrageous thought. Jane was the only woman on the *Celestial*, and besides a single crew member, the only survivor, right? They thought he was from the *Celestial*, but who knows?" She lowered her voice to a whisper. "What if *Polly* survived, not Jane? What if we're descended from a *pirate*?"

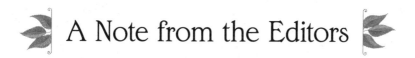 # A Note from the Editors

WE HOPE YOU ENJOYED ANOTHER exciting volume in the Miracles & Mysteries of Mercy Hospital series, published by Guideposts. For over seventy-five years, Guideposts, a nonprofit organization, has been driven by a vision of a world filled with hope. We aspire to be the voice of a trusted friend, a friend who makes you feel more hopeful and connected.

By making a purchase from Guideposts, you join our community in touching millions of lives, inspiring them to believe that all things are possible through faith, hope, and prayer. Your continued support allows us to provide uplifting resources to those in need. Whether through our online communities, websites, apps, or publications, we strive to inspire our audiences, bring them together, and comfort, uplift, entertain, and guide them.

To learn more, please go to guideposts.org.

Find more inspiring stories in these best-loved Guideposts fiction series!

Mysteries of Lancaster County

Follow the Classen sisters as they unravel clues and uncover hidden secrets in Mysteries of Lancaster County. As you get to know these women and their friends, you'll see how God brings each of them together for a fresh start in life.

Secrets of Wayfarers Inn

Retired schoolteachers find themselves owners of an old warehouse-turned-inn that is filled with hidden passages, buried secrets, and stunning surprises that will set them on a course to puzzling mysteries from the Underground Railroad.

Tearoom Mysteries Series

Mix one stately Victorian home, a charming lakeside town in Maine, and two adventurous cousins with a passion for tea and hospitality. Add a large scoop of intriguing mystery, and sprinkle generously with faith, family, and friends, and you have the recipe for *Tearoom Mysteries*.

Ordinary Women of the Bible

Richly imagined stories—based on facts from the Bible—have all the plot twists and suspense of a great mystery, while bringing you fascinating insights on what it was like to be a woman living in the ancient world.

To learn more about these books, visit Guideposts.org/Shop